COVENANTS ON CAMPUS

Covenant Discipleship Groups
for
College and University Students

Kim A. Hauenstein-Mallet
Kenda Creasy Dean

DISCIPLESHIP RESOURCES
MATERIALS FOR GROWTH IN CHRISTIAN FAITH AND LIFE
P.O. Box 189 • Nashville, TN 37202 • Phone (615) 340-7284

Unless otherwise indicated, all scripture quotations are taken from the New Revised Standard Version of the Holy Bible.

ISBN 0-88177-099-X

Library of Congress Catalog Card No. 90-62152

DR099B

CONTENTS

Appendices

PREFACE

This book has been a national effort. Covenant Discipleship group leaders from all over the country have responded to questionnaires in a very candid and helpful way. The book comes as a response to the request for further help in creating and sustaining Covenant Discipleship groups on campus.

Many gifts of thanks are in order. Primary among these is to David Lowes Watson, for unleashing the power of our Methodist heritage upon us with the Covenant Discipleship program, and to Phyllis Tyler-Wayman, who has nurtured and encouraged this resource for those who work with Covenant Discipleship groups in the unique setting of the college campus.

I also want to acknowledge the support of Ben Curry, campus minister at the University of Miami and national coordinator for the college Covenant Discipleship program. Ben's comments and suggestions as we developed this resource were most helpful.

Kenda Creasy Dean, whom I first met in 1977 when she was president of the East Ohio Conference Council on Youth Ministries, graciously agreed to write from her perspective as a campus minister on the staff of University United Methodist Church in College Park, Maryland. Kenda wrote Chapter 2 and Chapter 13 of the manuscript.

Craig Gallaway and Stephen Potter of Discipleship Resources have provided excellent advice concerning the revision and promotion of the manuscript. Their assistance has been valuable to me and is appreciated.

Lorraine Hauenstein-Mallet was the proofreader for the original manuscript. Lorraine deserves thanks for her patient and thorough work. As a member of a Covenant Discipleship group, Lorraine was also able to make several suggestions that helped to clarify portions of the book.

I am grateful to those involved with campus Covenant Discipleship groups who responded to the questionnaire that provided us with national data and helped direct the writing of this manuscript: Ben Curry; Kathryn Pigg of Sam Houston State University in Huntsville, Texas; Kenda Creasy Dean and Kathleen Kline-Chesson of the University of Maryland in College Park; Marty J. Hamrick of West Texas State University in Canyon; Jim Nelson of Drake University in Des Moines, Iowa; Wade A. Holland of the University of Mississippi in University; Ann Hunt of the University of California at Santa Cruz; Scott Wilkinson, formerly of Wayne State University in Detroit, Michigan; David Danley of High Point College in High Point; Richard E. Coldwell of Ohio Northern University in Ada; Kenneth L. Wallace of Southern Illinois University in Carbondale; and Peter Booth, Noma Ladendorff, Kelly Lawrence, Lisa Ladendorff, Stacy Gordon, and Stacey Kidman at the University of Arizona in Tucson.

I am not easily won to new church programs. But I am overwhelmed by what I see happening in the lives of college students as the result of weekly participation in a Covenant Discipleship group where all members "watch over each other in love."

Kim Hauenstein-Mallet
United Methodist Campus Minister
University of Arizona, Tucson
October 1, 1990

INTRODUCTION

*It has always been difficult to sustain a
faithful Christian witness in the world, because
the world is not yet the kingdom of God.*[1]

Campus ministers know that the college campus today can
be a place of loneliness and isolation, just as it was at Oxford
University in the time of John Wesley. For a student who seeks to
work out his or her Christian values, the atmosphere on campus
can provide a challenge. For many students, there is no support
system unless they can find a friend who shares their faith. Even
then, they might have difficulty finding a support group that will
help them nurture and strengthen important values.

The task of campus ministry and of student ministry in local
churches is to discover how to reach out to college and university
students in ways that will not only support their faith development,
but also challenge them to live out their faith in the world outside
the campus setting. Higher education involves more than simply
what a student learns from classes on campus. Yet the specializa-
tion of academic disciplines, especially in the large campus and
university settings, gives an ever narrowing focus to the "real
world" of the student. Edward Farley has framed the situation
this way:

> What do we mean by an educated person? I can offer only some brief
> suggestions as to what we might mean—what a modern version of the Greek
> *paideia* might be. Consider the following five marks. (1) An educated person
> is sufficiently exposed to a plurality of experiences and modes of interpreta-
> tion to be self-conscious in his or her responses, decisions, and policies. (2)
> This self-consciousness has a critical dimension. It is self-consciousness
> about evidence and what constitutes the establishment of a claim or the
> grounding of a tradition or policy. (3) This critical attitude reflects the
> capacity to look beyond things and beneath things, to respond not just to
> surfaces and face values. (4) The educated person is self-conscious in his or

her general existence in society, in the exercise of discerned obligation. In other words, the person knows enough about the workings of local and larger societies to interpret critically issues of social praxis. (5) The educated person is sufficiently introduced to the heritage of cultural accomplishments (say, in literature, music, and the arts) to enjoy aesthetic dimensions of experience beyond those which are commercially and faddishly orchestrated.[2]

The challenge to campus ministry and to the church is to provide the linkage between book-knowledge and a more rounded and complete form of knowledge. The challenge to the church is to discover who the students are on campus and how they can relate to the congregation. Then the church can decide how to provide students with the best possible opportunities to explore their values with others who share their faith concerns.

Those of us who are interested in campus ministry have learned that the "boundaries" for ministry are growing. We cannot separate ourselves from the local church. In almost every local church, we know there is a "hidden student population." This fact has been brought about by the community college, which serves students of all ages. Among these students are second-career people, single parents, and a variety of individuals in addition to students who have just graduated from high school. These nontraditional students do not usually live on campus. They live throughout our communities. They attend local churches. Because they do not "look like students," many church members do not even realize they are there. Yet these students are in need of the church's ministry. Students who do not fit the traditional age group and who do not live in traditional student housing usually experience increased tensions. The local church is in a unique position to offer these students what they need for faith development at this critical time in their lives. The campus minister is in a unique position to provide resources and expertise for this ministry. This will be the focus of Chapter 4.

Campus ministry centers are also in a desirable position to serve the spiritual needs of the student population. In this book, several options will be explored for supporting students in their faith journey through the use of the Covenant Discipleship group program. This program works well in ecumenical campus ministry settings, in campus ministry that is done in connection with a local church, or even in alternative settings such as the student union or a dormitory room. It serves the needs of the student who is lookng for a group on campus that shares her or his values. It appeals to students who are willing to do "something more" in terms of their faith but have not found a challenge which has captured their imagination.

Further, the Covenant Discipleship group program creates a core of student leaders in your campus ministry program. The detailed appendices in this book are intended primarily for students who accept leadership responsibilities after participating in a pilot group for one year. By following the guidelines presented in the text and in the appendices, students can build confidence in their leadership abilities as they lead their peers in the Covenant Discipleship group experience.

Lisa Grant, author of *Branch Groups: Covenant Discipleship for Youth,* is correct when she says, "There is, today, a sincere and intense felt need for spiritual formation and discipleship."[3] And when David Lowes Watson says that many in our churches "are willing and ready to make a commitment to a reliable and faithful discipleship,"[4] he is describing many students on our college and university campuses today. Religious studies classes throughout the country are experiencing overflow registrations. Campus ministers from every section of the country are reporting growth and new excitement among students who participate in their ministries.

Covenant Discipleship groups provide us with the opportunity to offer students a challenge that will not only provide them with meaning on their religious pilgrimage now, but will help them become leaders in the church for the twenty-first century.

Part One:
MODELS FOR DISCIPLESHIP

I. A Discipleship Model: Jesus of Nazareth

Much in modern biblical scholarship suggests that the model for accountable discipleship, which we will discuss in these pages, is not alien to a model shared by Jesus with his disciples. In the New Testament writings, the ministry of Jesus is not recorded, of course, until well after his death.[5]

Nevertheless, certain patterns emerge from the New Testament record that are found acceptable to the broad spectrum of biblical analysts and scholars. For our purposes, the identification of these patterns is all that is necessary to describe memorable parts of Jesus' ministry that compare favorably and directly to what happens in Covenant Discipleship groups.

For our basis, we claim the following three tenets as basic to the ministry of Jesus:

1. A pattern of regular spiritual discipline, including worship and personal devotion
2. Public teaching, which equipped others for discipleship
3. A dynamic discipleship that included works of justice and compassion

These three tenets are basic to the New Testament record and were instrumental to the understandings of John Wesley concerning the Christian life. More will be said about this in the second chapter. In Chapter 3, the Covenant Discipleship model developed by David Lowes Watson will display the same three principles as basic to Christian discipleship today.

REGULAR SPIRITUAL DISCIPLINE
Worship and Devotion

The New Testament writers, while proclaiming Jesus to be the Christ, certainly did not have to prove his spirituality or his use of

3

the personal spiritual disciplines. Those things might have been assumed of the Son of God.

Still, the writers of the Gospels place Jesus regularly in the synagogue. Also, even though the account of Jesus' ministry is an account of his public activity, there are several accounts of times when Jesus went away alone to pray.

Again, prayer might have been assumed of Jesus, but the fact that the New Testament writers identified "times alone" indicates that even the Son of God needed time for personal spiritual discipline. This is not insignificant. In Covenant Discipleship, the spiritual disciplines will be identified as prayer, worship, searching the scriptures, regular participation in Holy Communion and the ministry of the Word, and fasting or bodily discipline.

For the busy pastor, student, or business person who never takes a day off, it is necessary to hear that Jesus would, at times, "withdraw to deserted places and pray."[6] For harried college students who have so many demands on their time already, it is necessary to be reminded that Jesus "went out to a deserted place, and there he prayed."[7] And for modern Christians who feel guilty for wanting to take time for themselves, it is important to note that Jesus "went up the mountain by himself to pray."[8]

Time for devotion and worship is one of the three basic tenets for Christian discipleship.

EQUIPPING OTHERS FOR DISCIPLESHIP
The C.D.G. Meeting

Jesus was called "rabbi" or teacher. One of the aspects of his teaching was to help individuals increase their faith in God and their understanding of the divine purpose for their lives.

To the masses, Jesus taught most memorably in terms of simple stories, called parables, which held immense spiritual insights for his hearers. Marianne Moore once described the parables as "imaginary gardens with real toads in them."[9] Jesus used parables in public because many times he would be speaking to groups that included the scribes and Pharisees, who considered themselves a bit too self-righteous, as well as outcasts and sinners, who were despised by Jesus' religious contemporaries. Through the use of parables, Jesus masterfully told a single story that spoke a message of judgment to the self-righteous and, at the same time, a message of hope and grace to the outcast. Unlike a lecture, which is soon identified by the hearer as such, allowing the listener to turn it off, these wonderful little stories seemed to draw people into them. Then, at a crucial time, the unmistakable point was made and individuals were surprised to find that the interesting little story was, in fact, a word of personal judgment or grace.

Through the parable, Jesus spoke a word that was understandable and applicable to his hearers in direct relation to their religious faith. His public teaching was for that purpose: to help individuals understand, develop, and demonstrate their religious faith. Even with the smaller group of disciples, Jesus' teaching aimed at this purpose.

Norman Perrin has written of the tremendous impact of the table fellowship Jesus shared with his closest disciples.[10] This table fellowship culminated in the Last Supper, but it was a significant part of his entire public ministry, as well. Jesus would meet with this tiny band of disciples regularly and, while breaking bread together, he would teach them the meaning of the spiritual disciplines and of discipleship. These teachings became the basis of the public ministry of the disciples as they developed the early Christian church.

The Covenant Discipleship group meeting, which consists of two to seven persons, also aims at this purpose: to bring increased accountability to the personal spiritual disciplines in such a way that they become the basis for Christian action in the world. Meeting together in an intimately small group to develop personal spiritual disciplines is a second tenet of Christain discipleship.

DYNAMIC DISCIPLESHIP—SERVICE TO OTHERS
Works of Justice and Compassion

When they had finished breakfast, Jesus said to Simon Peter, "Simon son of John, do you love me more than these?" He said to him, "Yes, Lord; you know that I love you." Jesus said to him, "Feed my lambs." A second time he said to him, "Simon son of John, do you love me?" He said to him, "Yes, Lord; you know that I love you." Jesus said to him, "Tend my sheep." He said to him the third time, "Simon son of John, do you love me?" . . . And he said to him, "Lord, you know everything; you know that I love you." Jesus said to him, "Feed my sheep. Very truly, I tell you, when you were younger, you used to fasten your own belt and to go wherever you wished. But when you grow old, you will stretch out your hands, and someone else will fasten a belt around you and take you where you do not wish to go" (John 21:15-18).

It is not necessary to assign any single literal meaning to this passage from John 21 in order to grasp its more general meaning to those who wrote the Gospels: The public ministry of Jesus included a theme on reaching out to others in the name of Christ, regardless of the cost of such discipleship, and even when that outreach would carry the individual "where you do not wish to go."

The meaning of that passage could not have been misunderstood in the early church, which by the time John was writing his Gospel, was already well aware of the horror of the Roman persecution. Even in the face of that atrocity, the theme of Christian discipleship was clear: It was to include a ministry of outreach to others regardless of the personal consequences.

"Works of Justice and Compassion," which are an integral part of the covenant developed by each Covenant Discipleship group, are not intended to help that group become a "mini missions committee." Rather, these works are seen as an integral part of individual discipleship required of each group member and are expressed in a way best suited to individual group members. The works of justice and compassion include efforts to understand and minister to others in need.

Outreach is a third tenet of Christian discipleship.

CONCLUSION

The New Testament record concerning the public ministry of Jesus would suggest at least the following three aspects to Jesus' teaching concerning discipleship: development of personal spiritual disciplines (including devotion and worship), meeting together regularly for conversation to develop and sustain discipleship, and reaching out to others in justice and compassion.

We will now see how these three tenets influenced John Wesley's understanding of Christian discipleship.

II. "Watch Over Each Other in Love": John Wesley's Model for Discipleship

Kenda Creasy Dean

A society is no other than a company of men [and women] having the form and seeking the power of godliness, united in order to pray together, to receive the word of exhortation, and to watch over one another in love, that they may help each other to work out their salvation (From John Wesley's *Rules of the United Societies*, 1743).

The first tragedy to affect me personally was the news that my sister had multiple sclerosis. I staggered under the weight of the diagnosis and the dreams it altered. Overcome by my own powerlessness, I bewailed my frustration to a friend from seminary. "I have no coping skills for this. Eventually I've got to learn to cope with this."

"Will you stop talking about 'coping skills'!" my friend finally exclaimed. "There are no 'coping skills' that will make this acceptable. What you need is a transformation. If you're going to help her, you're going to have to let God transform you."

She wasn't talking about an overnight, experiential change. She meant the ongoing submission of clay to a potter; the necessity of being pounded and kneaded till the potter deems the clay workable; of being precisely centered on the spinning wheel to avoid distortion; of being shaped slowly into something useful "by the strong, steady pressure brought to bear in the course of hundreds, perhaps thousands, of revolutions of the wheel."[11] This existing pot of mine was too shallow to hold such news as my sister's. It was useless to her. Only breaking it down and remolding it into a different vessel with deeper wells could help her . . . or me.

Such remolding means submission to the Potter-God, whose

7

grace breaks down and builds up anew in the thousands of revolutions of daily life. Few theologians knew the formative power of the Potter-God better than John Wesley, whose own life was broken down and recast on the potter's wheel many times in his long and remarkable ministry. It is no wonder that Wesley's model for following Christ—corporate discipleship—was for ordinary people struggling against daily distractions to remain perfectly centered on the wheel, in order to become the creation the Potter had in mind.

This kind of submission to the Potter-God is difficult. It runs contrary to human will and certainly to Western culture. Wesley recognized that Christian discipleship—so simple in principle, yet demanding in practice—was a Herculean task for the most pious of priests, much less for the rank and file Christian. Therefore, in Wesley's model for discipleship, Christians were to "watch over one another in love, that they may help each other to work out their own salvation." In other words, through corporate discipleship we assist the Potter-God by keeping the clay moist and responsive to the subtle pressures of the Potter-God's hands as they transform us into useful vessels. Wesley called these subtle pressures the "promptings and warnings of the Holy Spirit," and the method he devised for responding to them was known as the "class meeting."

THE ORIGINS OF THE CLASS MEETING

Of course, corporate discipleship had a long and successful history before Wesley popularized it with the class meeting. Monastic communities had long relied on community norms for spiritual formation. The pietistic Moravians, whose spiritual liveliness so impressed John and Charles Wesley, fine-tuned communal discipline into small "bands" of believers who scrutinized each other's souls with happy vengeance.[12] The Wesleys' own religious awakening was nurtured by their participation in supportive groups of believers. The Holy Club at Oxford and later the Fetter Lane Society and the group meeting on Aldersgate Street all played pivotal roles in their own spirituality.

By the eighteenth century, ritualistic rigidity and institutionalism had left the Church of England gasping for air and renewal. Against this background, the evangelistic preaching of

George Whitefield, John Wesley, and others found ready hearers among the industrial classes of Britain, whose poverty and despair were all but ignored by the Church of England. The evangelistic gospel of "new birth" was elixir to the masses coming to terms with their pathetic social conditions. When the Anglicans formally evicted the loyal but overly "enthusiastic" Wesleys from their pulpits, John and his brother Charles took to the fields and mines with their hymn singing and preaching, appealing for spiritual conversion and social transformation in anyone who would listen.

But John Wesley realized that preaching alone could not produce mature disciples, and he began to develop corporate discipleship as a form of nurture for those who were won by preaching. Borrowing from the Moravians, he established small bands of Christians who held one another accountable not for their *belief,* but for their *behavior* as disciples. The bands were confidential, same-sex groups of five to eight men or women who met weekly for prayer, singing, testimony, and mutual examination of the state of one another's soul.

Soon the Wesleyan bands were overshadowed by the larger and more organized "Methodist societies," and as the societies grew too large for mutual examination and nurture, the class meetings emerged. Although similar in purpose to the band, class meetings were slightly larger, consisted of (and were led by) both men and women who held meetings in their homes. Most important, the class meeting—unlike the band—was open to "seekers," persons with religious doubts or questions, but who nonetheless "desired to flee from the wrath to come, and to be saved from their sins."[13] It is easy to see how the class meeting's geographical flexibility, lay leadership, and doctrinal openness led to an explosion of "Methodism" both in Britain and in America throughout the eighteenth and early nineteenth centuries.

Wesley was unwilling to allow the Methodist class meeting to deteriorate into the intensely inward spirituality of the Moravians, however. So in 1743 he composed *The Rules of the United Societies* (Appendix G, page 86), outlining the disciple's expected behavior as a lover of both God and neighbor. The rules indicate that members should "continue to evidence their desire for salvation" in three general ways. First, they were to do no harm and avoid

evil. Second, they were to do good to all people as they had the
opportunity. Third, they were to attend "upon all the ordinances
of God."

Having agreed to submit to these guidelines, made more
specific by the addition of Wesley's own suggestions (e.g., refrain-
ing from "uncharitable and unprofitable conversation," "giving
food to the hungry and cloathing to the poor," and attending the
"publick worship of God"), each disciple was examined by the class
leader. At each meeting, the following five questions were asked of
everyone:

- What known Sin have you committed since our last meeting?
- What Temptation have you met with?
- How were you delivered?
- What have you thought, said, or done of which you doubt whether it be Sin
  or not?
- Have you nothing you desire to be kept secret?[14]

It has been suggested that these questions point more to
Wesley's need to control than to his desire for discipleship, but
Wesleyan scholar David Lowes Watson argues that this accusation
misunderstands the purpose of the class meeting. "The point at
issue . . . was whether justifying faith occasioned merely a formal
change in the believer or was the beginning of a substantive
change occasioned by . . . a new relationship with God."[15] In
short, Wesley intended the class meeting to do more than develop
"coping skills" for Christians. The class meeting was to serve as a
vehicle for transformation—a means of staying at the center of the
wheel so the Potter-God could mold believers into new and useful
creations.

CORPORATE DISCIPLESHIP
A Cord of Three Strands

The genius of Wesley's brand of corporate discipleship was less
what it stressed about discipleship than *how* it stressed it. In his
Rules for the United Societies (1743), Wesley defined a society as
"having the form and seeking the power of godliness." In other
words, Wesley considered the very form of the society itself—the
small group—a means of grace, possessing the "power of godliness."

One of the distinctive features of Wesley's model for discipleship and what accounted for its stunning success in spreading the Wesleyan movement was its understanding of *community* as a means of grace:

> Two are better than one. . . . If one falls down, his friend can help him up. But pity the man who falls and has no one to help him up! Also, if two lie down together, they will keep warm. But how can one keep warm alone? Though one may be overpowered, two can defend themselves. A cord of three strands is not quickly broken (Ecclesiastes 4:9-12, NIV).

To be a Christian is to be called into community. To Wesley, the community mediated grace in three ways. First, the class meeting intentionally worked toward the transformation of its members. The purpose of the class meeting was for members to "watch over one another in love, that they may help each other work out their salvation." To Wesley, salvation was a lifelong process of sanctification, one's transformation into the likeness of God, the reshaping of clay into a new vessel that holds nothing (consciously) but love. The class meeting fostered nurture, study, encouragement, stewardship, witness, and service to this end. All of these needed to be present in the life of any believer, and Wesley saw that they were best mediated through the group experience.[16]

Second, the class meeting was a means of grace because the Christian group is, by nature, incarnational. Because Christian fellowship embodies the clear and present nearness of God, Christ's transforming power—instituted in the sacraments and holy teachings of the church—could be *experienced* "where two or three are gathered." And one's experience of this grace has transforming power:

> Groups offer settings wherein a tremendous measure of spiritual guidance happens in quite ordinary ways. They provide a direct, intense, interpersonal environment where we learn from watching how others negotiate the Christian life. . . . Authentic intimacy is transformational in character, partly because we discover . . . that reality "out there" is not indifferent to our presence. . . . When face-to-face groups flourish, there exists a greater possibility for creativity in Christian care. Christian love makes ordinary people extraordinary in their responses to one another.[17]

Naturally, when ordinary people are made extraordinary in their responses to each other, not only is their relationship with

God transformed; so is their relationship with one another. Thus, the class meeting mediated grace in yet a third way: through social concern for the unfortunate neighbor. The earliest societies spawned hospitals and schools and outreach of every kind; their influence had been credited (and exaggerated) for saving England from revolutionary upheaval and with reducing the national alcoholism level.[18] Both in England and in America, one of the earliest hallmarks of a Methodist was his or her concern for relentless social action.

CONCLUSION

But the significance of the class meeting was not its social impact, despite Wesley's call to "do all the good you can."[19] The class meeting's real importance and appeal lay in the witness it bore to Jesus Christ through the faithful obedience of Christian disciples. The development of the class meeting was crucial to the spread of the Wesleyan movement, but not only because it touched many lives. What was so powerful about corporate discipleship was that, through the mutual admonition and encouragement of the class meeting, corporate discipleship helped transform those lives and set them on fire. In spirit and in structure, the class meeting was faithful to the New Testament portrayal of Jesus and his call for disciples. In practice, the personal piety and community outreach engendered by the class meeting resulted in a spiritually awakened, socially responsive body of believers whose testimony celebrated being shaped by the Potter-God:

> Here then to thee thy own I leave;
> Mould as thou wilt thy passive clay:
> But let me all thy stamp receive;
> But let me all thy words obey,
> Serve with a single heart and eye,
> And to thy glory live and die.[20]

III. A Discipleship Model for Today: Covenant Discipleship

W e have seen in the previous chapters a triad of themes for discipleship, which come down to us not only from the time of John Wesley and the early Methodist movement, but from gleanings from the New Testament record of the life of Jesus and the early Christian movement. These three themes include an emphasis on personal and corporate devotion, "conversation" with other Christian pilgrims for accountability and support, and concern about the social order leading to works of outreach for justice and compassion.

These are the three marks of the Covenant Discipleship group. David Lowes Watson, in his book *Covenant Discipleship: Christian Formation Through Mutual Accountability,* describes how these three themes work together in the modern Christian life:

> We have found personal forgiveness and reconciliation in Christ, as have countless others. But now our call to discipleship sends us back into the world where we are confronted very directly with the realities of sin, suffering, and evil which make our personal sin pale by comparison. For now we see sin and suffering are not just personal but global and systemic. Now we are much more aware of the injustice of oppression, the torment of disease, the scandal of starvation, and the cheapness of human life.
>
> In other words, the joy and the freedom of personal discipleship lead us inexorably to the challenge of global discipleship. And the question that now presses us is, How can we be obedient to Jesus Christ in a world that remains rebellious against God, not least because we still find rebellious tendencies in ourselves? [21]

With that description, it is not surprising that Covenant Discipleship groups find an interested audience among college and university students. Over the past two years, I have had several opportunities to meet with groups of from 25 to 150 campus ministers at various meetings and seminars. On campuses throughout the United States, the major concerns being raised by students at the beginning of the 1990s are primarily these: saving the environment, building understanding among people of different cultural and racial backgrounds, and identifying local service projects and becoming involved as volunteers (this, in spite of the fact that many full-time students are also working part-time or full-time in addition to studying).

Moreover, students appear to be committed to faith development as the foundation for their own participation as Christian disciples in the global community. Being part of a Covenant Discipleship group is an excellent way to work at a full and balanced faith development process. Such a process should include works of justice and compassion as well as devotion and worship, disallowing an imbalance toward one or the others and monitoring spiritual growth by the means of grace offered through Christian conversation in a sympathetic, focused, supportive group.

Not all college and university students are seeking the additional commitments that come with a Covenant Discipleship group. But in every local church and on every campus where I have associated with post-high school students, I have always found some who were asking for "something more" to help them with their personal faith and Christian discipleship. *If there are two such students in your church or campus ministry unit, you already have a pilot Covenant Discipleship group ready to start.*

There are also indications that Covenant Discipleship groups might fill an important role in campus ministry when students are away from their home church. Whereas the national data show that 10 to 15 percent of the membership of a local church might become involved in the Covenant Discipleship program, 35 percent of our active students in the United Methodist Campus Ministry at the University of Arizona are involved in a Covenant Discipleship group in addition to other campus ministry activities and regular church attendance. This seems like a high percentage, and not all the reasons for participation have been discovered. The most obvious reason, however, is that the Covenant Discipleship group is meeting an important need in the lives of those students.

THE PERSONAL DISCIPLINES ON CAMPUS

The idea of the "practice of the presence of God"[22] is one that interests and challenges many students as a model for personal discipleship. John Wesley's model for discipleship seems much like it: a regular effort to remind oneself of the requirements of the Christian life. In turn, when we remember and endeavor to fulfill the requirements of Christian discipleship, we receive grace and understand what Jesus meant when he said, "I came that they may have life, and have it abundantly."[23] When we fail to meet these disciplines, we are often caught up in the busyness of life and might feel emptiness as a result. "The perfection which Wesley regarded as attainable in this life was thus one of mature discipleship, a relationship to God in which obedience had become so habitual that the will had lost its tendency to resist the sovereignty of grace."[24]

The early Methodists, then, followed the "General Rules of the Methodist Societies" and believed God's grace was brought to them as the religious disciplines were practiced. The works of piety were listed as follows: prayer (private, family, and public), searching the scriptures, the sacrament of the Lord's Supper, public worship, fasting or bodily discipline, and Christian fellowship. The works of mercy are summarized as: not to sin against God and one's neighbor, and to do all the good one can for God and one's neighbor.

In Covenant Discipleship groups, the works of piety and mercy are incorporated into what Watson calls the General Rule of Discipleship: "To witness to Jesus Christ in the world, and to follow his teachings through acts of compassion, justice, worship, and devotion, under the guidance of the Holy Spirit."[25]

Covenant Discipleship group members are challenged to regularly include the four aspects of the General Rule as a part of their lives. The covenant developed by the group is a balance of the four. Sample covenants may be found in Appendix D (p. 75).

THE GROUP MEETING

Christian fellowship is listed as one of the means of grace in the "General Rules of the United Societies." In the Covenant Discipleship model, the individual is accountable on a weekly basis to the members of her or his Covenant Discipleship group. Once the members have worked together to develop the clauses of a covenant, representing the goals of their corporate life, the covenant itself becomes the main agenda for the weekly meeting.

Jesus met with the disciples in what New Testament scholar Norman Perrin calls the "table fellowship."[26] Wesley encouraged class meetings among the members of the societies, and he personally met regularly with the "select society, in which the doctrine of Christian perfection was most demonstrably experienced and practiced. . . . He also looked upon them as a 'select company, to whom I might unburden myself on all occasions, without reserve; and whom I could propose to all their brethren as a pattern of love, of holiness, and of good works.'"[27]

The weekly Covenant Discipleship group meeting fulfills a similar need on the modern campus. It allows students to gather regularly for conversation with other students who share their Christian goals and values.

As these students meet together, something else happens, something not unlike Wesley's finding. Watson writes that "class leaders . . . became as skilled a group of spiritual mentors as the church has ever produced. What Wesley looked for in a leader was a combination of disciplinary and spiritual discernment, so that fellowship in the classes would be a means of growing discipleship."[28] Such a process occurs in the Covenant Discipleship group. As persons grow in discipleship, they develop as leaders and spiritual mentors in the church for years to come.

CAMPUS OUTREACH

The Covenant Discipleship group is not meant to become a social outreach committee. As Watson writes about the early Methodist class meeting: "We must look to the class meeting, not as a paradigm for Christian witness for the world—for that was its effect—but rather as a means of seeking obedience to God's will— for that was its purpose."[29]

Covenant Discipleship group members are highly likely to become involved with organized groups and programs for social outreach and healing. But this is the *effect* of the weekly meeting, not the primary purpose.

To go out into a hurting world or onto a hurting campus without being discouraged or bitter, students need to be able to return, at times, to a "home base." That home base can be the weekly Covenant Discipleship meeting, where others are working on the same goals in the same hostile environment and will understand how difficult it is because they share the same values and share the same source of hope.

Jesus instituted the Lord's Supper for the disciples to come back to home base for encouragement, reporting, understanding, and support. Wesley instituted the class meeting for similar purposes. The weekly class meetings were described as the "'sinews' of the Methodist movement, the means by which members 'watched over one another in love.'"[30]

The Covenant Discipleship group meeting does this for the modern college student on a weekly basis. What follows in this book is an account of how Covenant Discipleship groups might be developed for college and university students. These groups may be developed by campus ministry units or by those in local churches who have identified and seek to nurture their student population.

Part Two:
HOW TO FORM A COLLEGE COVENANT DISCIPLESHIP GROUP

IV. Knowing Our Audience: Our Opportunity Among College Students

One of the most invisible and silent populations in the church today is that of college students. One reason for this is that students don't always "look like" students anymore. More and more students in our universities and community colleges are not fitting into the traditional student population, between eighteen and twenty-two years of age, and living in dormitories on campus.

The average student population is getting older, and it often includes second-career people. With the growth of the community college system, many students are members of local churches many miles from campus, even in traditionally rural areas. Even in a large university, off-campus living is the norm. At the University of Arizona in Tucson, 25,000 of the 37,000 students live in off-campus housing.

The result of these changes is that *students may be found in almost every local church.* In areas where campus ministry has been separated from the local churches, this fact offers the campus minister an opportunity to offer "consultant" services to local churches to establish Covenant Discipleship groups. The campus ministry is benefited in terms of increased support from the local church.

The campus minister can especially help the local church to identify and be sensitized to second-career students who may be older and in a time of transition. The church can become an important means of support to such students.

Also in many local churches are undergraduate students who are dealing with issues on campus in terms of their Christian faith. The church becomes a home base for receiving a Christian perspective on issues in higher education.

Because of their nature, focus, and adaptability to student schedules, Covenant Discipleship groups become an excellent

21

means of student involvement in Christian discipleship during college years.

LOCAL CHURCH STUDENT MINISTRY

Because local churches are increasingly identifying college students in their midst, many are attempting "student ministry" with these students.[31] One effective part of a student ministry can be Covenant Discipleship groups composed of two to seven students who meet regularly. Most often in a local church, a Covenant Discipleship group can meet on Sundays when students are more available.

CAMPUS MINISTRY UNITS

Covenant Discipleship groups are perfectly suited for the modern campus where students have difficult schedules including study, classes, and employment. Because the group can be as few as two and no more than seven members meeting at a mutually agreed time, scheduling a Covenant Discipleship group is easier than scheduling other student events that involve twenty-five or thirty students meeting at a single time and place. The ability to adapt Covenant Discipleship groups to flexible time schedules is a distinct advantage in the college setting.

Flexible locations also adapt well to the campus setting. At the University of Arizona, we have Covenant Discipleship groups meeting in five different settings, all successfully. One group meets before classes, at 7:00 A.M. around a table in a campus restaurant. Another meets in an apartment off campus on Fridays at 6:00 P.M., after members have finished their work day. Still another meets in a dormitory on campus on Monday evenings at 6:15 P.M. Two groups meet in a local church on Wednesdays at 4:45 P.M., immediately preceding the weekly dinner of the Wesley Fellowship. Another group meets in the same church on Fridays at noon, and one group meets at the Campus Christian Center on Sundays after worship. Following this Covenant Discipleship group meeting, the members of this group go to lunch together.

Other successful settings reported in a recent national survey include a Covenant Discipleship group in the religious life building at the University of Mississippi and at the student union and chapel at Ohio Northern University.

ECUMENICAL CAMPUS MINISTRIES

The Covenant Discipleship program can become ecumenical in at least two proven ways. In a campus ministry setting, students involved in a Covenant Discipleship group will often invite friends to take part in the group. Quite often, these friends are roommates who are from another denomination and give the Covenant Discipleship group an ecumenical emphasis.

In a more intentional way, Covenant Discipleship groups can be offered in an ecumenical campus center. This might begin with a Covenant Discipleship group consisting of campus ministers representing the various campus ministries, each of whom can then lead a group of ecumenical students. At the Campus Christian Center at the University of Arizona, the Episcopal Chaplain, John D. Kautz, has begun an ecumenical Covenant Discipleship group.

THE SPECIAL NATURE OF THE COMMUNITY COLLEGE

At the local community college, a Covenant Discipleship group can meet at lunch or reserve a room for the weekly meeting. With the limited on-campus time of community college students, it is best to recruit students *before* setting and announcing a meeting time for such a group. Other students who are on campus at that time and are interested could then join the group upon hearing or seeing the announcement, or a new group might be formed at an alternate time out of the membership of the existing group.

Another possible setting for a Covenant Discipleship group with community college students is the local church. Because many such students are pursuing a second career, attention might be given to child care in the attempt to recruit such a group. A key to the development of this group would be to discover who the students are in the congregation and then to determine whether the bond between those students can bring them together into a Covenant Discipleship group. Recruitment can be done by the person in the local church who is responsible for college-age ministries.

A REMINDER

Remember, *students are extremely busy.* This fact needs to be respected in any attempt to minister with them. Not many students are searching out new ways to spend their time. At the same time, average attendance at weekly Covenant Discipleship group meetings is over 90 percent. That indicates that students who become involved in the Covenant Discipleship program also become committed to it as something worthy of their time and commitment. But, again, students are not looking for something more to do.

For those who want to initiate a Covenant Discipleship program, more than announcement is required to make it a success. An *excitement* about the value of the program must be communicated. *Personal invitation* is, by far, the most effective recruitment technique. *Identification of students* (including nontraditional age students) is essential to begin programs in the local church setting. Finally, *opportunity* must be given for those students who are interested. The campus minister is the key to this, both in the campus ministry setting and as a consultant with local churches who wish to begin the Covenant Discipleship program as a part of their student ministry.

V. Introducing the Idea: The Pilot Group

Chances are, you know several students who seem to be seeking "something more" in terms of their Christian faith. I don't want to define it further. There are simply some students who participate in all—or most of—the activities of a campus ministry unit and still seem to be ready for more. Their energy, dedication, and commitment are unusually high.

Those are the students to contact personally when you decide to start a pilot Covenant Discipleship group. Write them a personal letter in which you describe the basic concept of Covenant Discipleship groups. Tell them about the high level of commitment that is required, and tell them you thought of them *because of* that requirement. Invite them to meet with you for an informational meeting concerning Covenant Discipleship groups, after which they can decide whether this program is suited to them. A sample letter for recruitment can be found in Appendix E, p. 82.

A pilot group of two to seven members will meet for a full year. During that time, all group members will learn the process of developing a covenant. Each member will discover how to lead a Covenant Discipleship group meeting through personal experience in the pilot group. You will become closely acquainted with each of these people, so that you will be able to determine who might be effective Covenant Discipleship group leaders when new groups are offered the following year.

Experience suggests that although you might be tempted to start additional groups after one semester of the pilot group, it is not recommended. Some campuses have tried it, but I have yet to hear from a person who hasn't wanted the pilot group to continue for the full year before starting new groups. If it is necessary to start a new group, form a second pilot group. Commit to meet with the group for the first four or five meetings to develop the covenant and to experience the agenda for the weekly meeting. Then turn responsibility over to the members of that group with the understanding that you are always available for consultation if they experience any problems.

The participants in a Covenant Discipleship group are your primary source for interpretation and exposure of the program to others on campus. At the beginning of our second year of Covenant Discipleship groups at the University of Arizona, I announced a group meeting for all who were interested in the program. The meeting was, for me, what we sometimes call a "learning experience." I had met earlier in the day with six student group leaders, and these leaders were ready to sign up two to six members for each of their groups. A total of four students (other than the leaders) attended that meeting. I wondered what we would do. I was shocked; the leaders were disappointed. One week later, by word of mouth and by sharing of their experiences, the six student leaders had recruited twenty-eight additional students. Six Covenant Discipleship groups began to meet within two weeks.

The pilot group is essential for the success of the program. Stay together for a year. Talk to others about the experience. Develop student leadership, which will provide both future group leaders and the basis for recruitment of other students in future years.

INITIAL MEETING WITH THE PILOT GROUP

What do you attempt to accomplish at the initial meeting with the prospective pilot group members?

You will want to describe the program and be candid about the level of commitment required. You will want to evoke a response from the individuals. Be ready to start the Covenant Discipleship pilot group within a week of that initial meeting. Thus, student schedules must have been set and must be coordinated with your schedule.

The initial meeting can begin with a brief presentation about the importance of the class meeting to early Methodists. Material for this presentation can be found in Watson's *The Early Methodist Class Meeting: Its Origins and Significance* and *Covenant Discipleship: Christian Formation Through Mutual Accountability.*

"Covenant Discipleship Group" is a paper that was developed for this initial meeting (Appendix B, p. 68). Following a presentation on Wesley and the early Methodist class meeting, give a brief overview of this paper and ask for questions or comments. Finally, you will want to determine which of the students at the meeting wish to be a part of the pilot Covenant Discipleship group and determine a regular time and place for the weekly meeting. Inform the pilot group members that work on the group covenant will begin at the first meeting.

Some students may feel uneasy about participating further in the program. For this reason, it may be wise to conclude the initial meeting with an inclusive act (such as refreshments for all) rather than with the formation of the pilot group.

VI. Writing the Covenant

The first task of the Covenant Discipleship group is to write the covenant they will use in their weekly meetings. This process might take several weeks, and it is not to be hurried. *Each covenant is to be original and unique to the group, not copied.* As the covenant is being written, group members begin to learn about each other and to appreciate each other.

The normal process of writing the covenant includes the following successive stages:

1. Brainstorm on clauses that should be a part of the covenant. Allow all members to mention things they think are important. This brainstorming can usually be completed in the first or second one-hour meeting of the group.

2. At the beginning of the second meeting, if not before, a copy of all the ideas from the brainstorming session should be in the hands of each group member. During the second session, group members begin to evaluate the clauses that were listed during the brainstorming. Some clauses might be removed from further consideration by common consent. Other important items may be added at this time. Clauses that are close to each other in content or purpose might be combined. This stage of the covenant development will usually take two to three weeks, depending upon the group.

3. For a clause to appear in the final group covenant, all members must agree on it. (Other provisions are made for individual clauses, as you will see below.) If any member objects to a certain clause, that person should not be unduly pressured to accept it. Persuasion is fair, but pressure is not. In such a case, that clause should be dropped. Because Covenant Discipleship group meetings are no longer than one

hour, the number of clauses included in the covenant should not be more than ten. Staying below this limit may require further combining or possibly choosing the top ten priority clauses. Most covenants, however, will contain fewer than ten clauses.

THE PARTS OF THE COVENANT

The group covenant consists of the following:

Preamble and Conclusion

The preamble and conclusion of the covenant are "personalizing marks" that allow group members to work out language that describes their purpose for meeting together and their openness to work in accordance with the promptings of the Holy Spirit. The preamble should serve as an introduction to the clauses of the covenant, and the conclusion should serve as a summary of the group's purpose in meeting weekly.

Required Clauses

Wesley said that the means of grace are the building blocks for faith development. Taken from the "General Rules of the Methodist Societies," certain clauses are required as the building blocks of the covenant.

Required clauses in each covenant must include what Watson calls "The General Rule of Discipleship: To witness to Jesus Christ in the world, and to follow his teachings through acts of compassion, justice, worship, and devotion, under the guidance of the Holy Spirit."[32]

Therefore, *each covenant must include clauses that specifically address the General Rule of Discipleship:*

1. Acts of compassion   *3. Acts of worship*
2. Acts of justice   *4. Acts of devotion*

THE GENERAL RULE OF DISCIPLESHIP

Works of Mercy

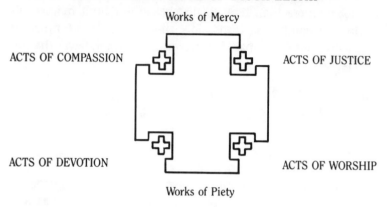

ACTS OF COMPASSION

ACTS OF JUSTICE

ACTS OF DEVOTION

ACTS OF WORSHIP

Works of Piety

As a group goes through the process of developing its covenant, it is a good idea for members to look at this list often to make
sure all the required clauses are being represented in the covenant. The way the clause is worked into the covenant is up to the
individual group.

Most groups find that it is not difficult to include devotion and
worship as part of the covenant, even though it is challenging to
perform these clauses on a regular basis.

In the national data collected for this book, one of the major
problems for Covenant Discipleship groups is finding worthwhile
and meaningful works of justice and compassion. As Lisa Ladendorff, a student Covenant Discipleship group leader at the University of Arizona, said, "Even though our clauses are balanced
between works of piety and works of mercy, I feel our acts of
compassion and justice involve too many safe things with people
(i.e., things we already do or people we already know)."

Finding ways to show compassion and encourage justice is a
common challenge to Covenant Discipleship groups, intensified by
student schedules, which often already include studies and employment. For this reason, it is important to mention some exciting things that are happening nationally as Covenant Discipleship
groups seek to discover meaningful opportunities for works of
mercy in their covenants.

Ben Curry, campus minister at the University of Miami and
national coordinator of college Covenant Discipleship groups, re-

ported, "We now have a weekly group of students who feed street people Sundays at 7:00 A.M., as an outgrowth of the Covenant Discipleship group." Kathleen Kline-Chesson of the University of Maryland in College Park reported that her Covenant Discipleship group performs acts of community service in Washington, D.C., including work at the Community Food Bank. A Covenant Discipleship group led by Peter Booth at the University of Arizona assists First United Methodist Church in the collection and delivery of food to the Tucson Community Food Bank.

Some groups, such as the group led by Marty Hamrick, campus minister at West Texas State University in Canyon, report that "students tend to do better at works of justice and compassion." Often, this includes peace with justice ministries. A clause in the covenant of the Covenant Discipleship group led by Jim Nelson, campus minister at Drake University in Des Moines, Iowa, is to "prayerfully work for justice in the world in which we live." Kathryn Pigg, campus minister at Sam Houston State University in Huntsville, Texas, reported, "One student's attitude toward social justice improved markedly through this experience. She was seminary-bound but not tuned in to social concerns."

Whatever challenges might be caused by the required clauses for acts of justice and compassion, the rewards appear to be worth the effort.

OPTIONAL, CONTEXTUAL CLAUSES

When each of the required clauses is represented, other clauses, which the entire group sees as important to its corporate discipleship, may be added to the covenant. These are called "optional" or "contextual" clauses.

OPEN CLAUSES

One or more members of the group might have a desire to work on some aspect of his or her discipleship, but the group members may not agree to include that particular clause as a part of the group covenant. When this happens, the individual makes a personal covenant with the group by sharing this "open clause" at the weekly meeting. The student is then accountable to the group at the following week's meeting.

THINGS TO REMEMBER WHEN WRITING
THE COVENANT

Because the weekly meeting is limited to one hour, remember to limit the number of clauses in the group covenant to ten or fewer. Each clause should be limited in scope and specific in expectations. Do not be too general. Specifics will allow group members to focus more on what they intend to do and to answer more clearly when the clauses are discussed.

When the covenant has been completed, a final copy is made for each group member. All copies of the covenant are passed around and signed by each of the other members.

Copies of sample covenants from active campus Covenant Discipleship groups may be found in Appendix D, p. 75.

VII. The Group Meeting

The weekly Covenant Discipleship group meeting is for no longer than one hour. The two to seven members of the group meet at the predetermined time and at a place that offers them enough privacy and intimacy to hold to their agenda in a way that meets the needs of all group members.

The main agenda of the meeting is the covenant itself. The method for using the group covenant in the weekly meeting is specific and very important. The group leader is responsible for questioning each group member, in turn, about his or her response to covenant. The leader then goes on to the next item in the covenant, questioning each member. This continues until each clause of the covenant is completed.

This catechetical approach to group process is different from a general group discussion process, and it needs to be recognized as such by the leader. Though some interaction may take place among the group members with supportive comments that seem appropriate and necessary at the time, *the Covenant Discipleship group is not to be thought of primarily as a support group.* Individual members report to the leader and to the group whether or not they have been successful in accomplishing the clauses of the covenant for that week. This is the primary and essential task to be completed at the weekly group meeting. Time for visiting, sharing, and personal agendas should come after the meeting or at another time during the week.

Therefore, the leadership model that has come to be associated with the Covenant Discipleship program must be diagrammed as in Figure 1. For comparison, Figure 2 shows the flow of conversation in a typical small group. You will notice that in the Covenant Discipleship model, the group leader is responsible for the questioning of individual group members and the flow of the meeting.

33

Figure 1   Figure 2

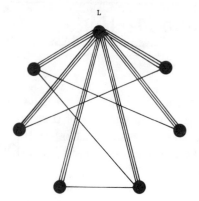
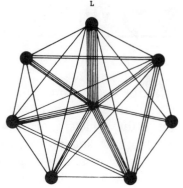

Flow of conversation in a   Flow of conversation in a
Covenant Discipleship group   typical small group
The catechetical process of   All of the members may
accountability gives the leader   interact, with the leader
a direct role   playing a nondirective role

OUTLINE OF A WEEKLY GROUP MEETING

1. The assigned leader for the week opens with a brief prayer.

2. The assigned leader immediately directs the attention of the group to the covenant, which is the main agenda for the meeting. Each member is then held accountable for her or his fulfillment of the covenant during the past week.

   a. The leader reads Clause 1 of the covenant and reports his or her own succeses and difficulties in that area. Then, one by one, group members are called upon to respond to Clause 1.

   b. The leader reads Clause 2 and follows the same procedure, followed by each remaining clause of the covenant.

   c. The assigned leader for the week is responsible to care for the group's time covenant for the weekly meeting by

      • Politely bringing to a close any lengthy statements, personal agendas, or tendencies toward gossip.
      • Disallowing in strong terms any statements that are judg-

mental or critical, and reminding members that this is not acceptable in a Covenant Discipleship group.

3. When the clauses of the covenant have been completed, the assigned leader asks for personal open clauses offered by individual group members the previous week. The individual then reports on his or her successes or difficulties with the personal open clause during that week.

4. The meeting agenda is then opened to individuals who have a personal open clause for which they wish to be held accountable during the next week.

5. Closing prayer is led by the assigned leader or a volunteer from the group.

6. Housekeeping matters for the following week:

   a. Assigned leader
   b. Agreed time and place for meeting
   c. Who will contact absentees

Except in highly unusual circumstances, there is no reason why the above steps cannot be accomplished by a group of seven persons in one hour.

If a group finds that its meetings are running longer than this, there are several possible reasons. Probably, the original group leader will need to refocus the group's attention on the covenant clauses and ask for responses and comments to be directed there. As the group members get to know each other better, there is an increased tendency toward words of encouragement, support, and even genuinely acceptable—and perceptively received—advice. The assigned leader for the week or the original group leader might find it necessary to remind the group at various times that the primary task of the Covenant Discipleship group is accountability to the covenant. Group members might be encouraged to meet afterwards or during the week to deal with personal agendas and needs.

A SAMPLE CONVERSATION IN A
CAMPUS COVENANT DISCIPLESHIP GROUP

LEADER: It's good to see you again. Let's have a brief prayer together as we begin. "God, in a few moments of silence, help us to leave behind the busyness of this day and realize that we are together again with each other and our covenant. (*Pause for a time of silence and centering*). Help each of us to be honest with each other and honest with you, trusting in your love for us and knowing we've not reached perfection and are always striving to be better people, in the Spirit of Christ. Amen."

Our first clause is, "I will try to see people who are difficult in my life as my teachers and to see other people in a nonjudgmental way."

Well, I have to admit I haven't done very well with that one this week. One very difficult person in my life is always challenging and seems to put me off guard. I need to keep working on that one.

Kelly, how did you do with that one?

KELLY: Well, I really worked hard on that clause this week. You know I've been having a rough time with my roommate. So I've really taken time to understand her this week and also to be quieter when I have to get up for an early class and she's still sleeping. I found that she's a lot more pleasant when I do that. So I've really been working hard on it, and I'm feeling better about it.

LEADER: Stacy?

STACY: Well, I was doing all right and then yesterday my lab partner gets on this kick about her boyfriend and how cute he is, and that's all she wants to talk about for three hours of lab. She keeps telling me all these things and saying, "Don't you think that's cute?" I really don't, but what do you say? I don't want to hurt her feelings, but I want to be honest, too. And I want to get my lab work done.

LISA: I know. I had a roommate like that once. All she ever wanted to do was to talk about her boyfriend, and I got tired of it so . . .

LEADER: Perhaps you two could get together later and share some ideas about how to resolve that. Greg, how did you do on this one?

GREG: Well, I think I did all right. I didn't have any real difficult people in my life this week, so I haven't had to think about it that much. But the things I was dealing with before—I think they're going okay.

LEADER: And Lisa?

LISA: Well, I've really had a hard time with this person who thinks his religion is all right and ours is all wrong. I mean, whenever we're out socially or something, everything is great. But when we start to talk to each other about religion, we're at each other's throats!

LEADER: So he is sort of judgmental about your religious faith?

LISA: *Sort of?* He thinks his church has the only right way, and I guess that makes me judgmental of him, really. I just keep trying to figure it out because I know we believe a lot of the same things. It's really hard to try to find Christian friends on campus who can let you be who you are.

LEADER: So you're learning something from this friend who is being judgmental of you?

LISA: Yeah. I can see how much it hurts the other person.

(Group continues through the other covenant clauses)

LEADER: Greg, you made a personal open clause with us last week about writing letters to parents and other people you care about. Can you report on that?

GREG: Yeah. I get so busy sometimes I think they must think I forgot them. So I wrote to my parents and my grandma. They really appreciated it. We talked on the phone this weekend. I just needed to do that.

LEADER: Does anyone have a personal open clause you'd like to be working on this week?

KELLY: I really like how my relationship with Tina, my roommate, is getting better. I want to make an open clause that I will be more considerate of her in the mornings this week.

LISA: I know about our clause about helping others by collecting food for the food bank, but I think I need to be doing something more. I'm going to make an open clause that I'll serve as a tutor to a child at an elementary school for an hour a week the rest of this semester.

LEADER: And you'll report back to us at our next meeting?

We normally close our group meeting with prayers for others. Do any of you have people in your life you'd like us to be thinking of and supporting with our prayers?

(Names are offered and listed by the leader. Each is named in closing prayers for others.)

Let us pray. O God, thank you for bringing us safely together again. Be with us now through another week. Help us with our devotion, worship, and our concerns for others in compassion and justice. Especially help us to be with these persons this week in prayer *(list of names mentioned)* so that we realize we are all one in Christ. Amen.

LEADER: We'll meet here again at 3:00 next week. We need a volunteer to be the assigned leader for that meeting. Does anyone want to lead?

KELLY: I'll lead next week.

LEADER: Okay. See you then.

VIII. The Significance of the Leader

When starting a pilot Covenant Discipleship group, the most important requirement for a leader is to experience a Covenant Discipleship group training seminar or to completely read one of the guidebooks for starting Covenant Discipleship groups.[33] The process outlined in these books may be followed to develop a group. Though the books do not allow for feedback and questions in the way training sessions do, a leader who wishes to begin a group by using one of these guidebooks may address questions to the Section on Covenant Discipleship at the General Board of Discipleship of The United Methodist Church, P. O. Box 840, Nashville, TN 37202-0840.

Once the covenant for the pilot group is written, usually from four to five weeks after the group begins to meet, the leadership of the weekly group meeting becomes a shared task. Group members take turns following the outline for the meeting, and the agenda for the meeting is the covenant itself (see Appendix A, p. 67). As the task is shared, however, there may be times when the original leader notices that the group process can be strengthened, and he or she should say so, clearly.

Some typical problems early in the group's life might include judgmentalism on the part of group members toward others, a tendency to abandon the covenant and enter into personal discussions, and an uncertainty or hesitancy on the part of the weekly leader concerning the group leadership style used in Covenant Discipleship groups. (This style was identified in Figure 1 in Chapter 7.) The original leader must be prepared to identify and address all these things.

Over the course of time, the group meeting process becomes second nature to group members, and leading the weekly group meeting becomes much easier. The original leader will be thinking about the future during this time, and she or he will attempt to identify persons in the group who might one day lead their own groups. As this "silent search" goes on, the leader will be keeping several qualities in mind. In this, John Wesley himself informed us.

Wesley looked for certain things in people he would later call to lead his Societies. "Wesley was aware that the authority of class leaders would depend to a large degree on the respect accorded by the class, not least because they were in touch with the members at precisely the point of accountability for discipleship. . . . [Class leaders] became as skilled a group of spiritual mentors as the church has ever produced. What Wesley looked for in a leader was a combination of disciplinary and spiritual discernment, so that fellowship in the classes would be a means of growing discipleship.[34]

These qualities make a very good basis for selecting Covenant Discipleship leaders today. During the course of the year, the original group leader will be getting an idea about which members of the pilot group are candidates. Sometime in the spring, probably about the time of the evaluation process, the group leader might want to speak to these candidates. Some may express interest; others, for very good reasons, may not want to assume the primary leadership responsibility for a Covenant Discipleship group. Either way, the program for the following fall can be planned on the basis of these contacts as well as the perceived interest among students who might be recruited as new group members in the Covenants on Campus program.

IX. Extending the Invitation

T he invitation to participate in a college Covenant Discipleship group is of great significance. Whereas Covenant Discipleship group members in local churches might continue together for years, the transient population on campus means that annual recruitment and replenishment with new members is essential.

For this reason, it is important for the "word to get out" about the Covenant Discipleship group program in as many ways as possible. It is still essential for the recruitment information to include candid information about the high level of commitment necessary. But on a busy campus, as perhaps in no other setting, it is critically necessary to extend the invitation to participate in every possible way.

DEVELOPMENT OF THE LEADERSHIP TEAM

In the pilot group, you will discover people who have the gifts of disciplinary and spiritual discernment Wesley looked for in his leaders. These people are naturals as you develop a leadership team for the development of the Covenants on Campus program.

By the end of the year in which the pilot group meets, you will want to share with each of these prospective group leaders your confidence in their skills and graces. Ask whether they might be willing to lead a Covenant Discipleship group the following fall. The response is usually positive. The rewards to the church are obvious: As these students take part in Covenant Discipleship groups and then become leaders, they are building skills that will continue to benefit their church participation throughout the future.

The leadership training aspect of the Covenants on Campus program is a by-product of the program, and a very important one! But it is much more than a by-product to the church in general, where the age group between eighteen and thirty represents the

41

largest group of individuals who become inactive in the church. At this critical time in the lives of young adults, the Covenant Discipleship program not only involves students, but it also gives them practical leadership training experience.

RECRUITMENT

When it comes time to form new groups, the leaders developed in the pilot group become by far the most important part of the recruitment process. Their sharing about "what happened to them" in the Covenant Discipleship group becomes an influence on friends, students, and groups with whom they associate. They will invite people they know—people who have already developed a level of trust with them—to be a part of their Covenant Discipleship group.

Other group members will join through means of open invitation, depending upon times that are most convenient to them. The open invitation extends to every student on campus who might want to participate. A brochure can be developed which gives a brief explanation of the Covenants on Campus program and the commitment involved. The brochure should have a response or registration form, which can be returned to you with the registrant's name, campus address, and telephone number. You or another group member may then contact that individual and invite him or her to the introductory session. Supplementary informational brochures can be ordered from the Covenant Discipleship section of the General Board of Discipleship in Nashville.

SETTING UP THE COVENANT DISCIPLESHIP GROUPS

After the pilot group has met for a year, with leaders for the following year identified and recruited, you will want to schedule a leadership training session for these new leaders very early in the new semester. We hold this session on the first Saturday morning of the semester and include a luncheon for the group leaders. The paper, "Covenant Discipleship Group" (see Appendix B, p. 68), can be used as the basis for this training session. These student leaders might then meet on a monthly basis with the program director to work out details and discuss issues from their group experience.

At the conclusion of the training session, the student group leaders identify a time and location convenient to them for their group meeting. These times are then offered to new group members at the introductory session. Adjustments may need to be made at that time, but for student volunteer leaders especially, the meeting time should be carefully negotiated. They will be giving a great deal of time in an already busy schedule; they cannot be expected to do so in a way that adversely affects their scholastic and personal lives.

A meeting for general information, the introductory session, is scheduled for students who have indicated a desire to participate in Covenant Discipleship groups through personal contact and other publicity. At this meeting, the "Covenant Discipleship Group" or something similar might be used (see Appendix B). The group leaders are then introduced. Sheets of newsprint with a different date, time, and location for each group might be placed on walls around the room, and at the conclusion of the introductory session, individuals may sign up for the various groups. A sheet is also provided for those who wish to participate but cannot find a time that will allow for their participation in any of the existing groups. Those who sign this additional sheet might meet with the program director at a mutually agreed upon time. Or, if one of the student group leaders has not recruited anyone for her or his group at this time, that leader might negotiate a new time with this group.

After hearing about the commitment required in a Covenant Discipleship group, some individuals may decide not to participate. It is important to help these people feel gracefully excused from the meeting. One way might be to break for refreshments as individuals are roaming around the room to sign up on the newsprint sheets.

It is recommended that Covenant Discipleship groups begin to meet in the week following the introductory session.

X. Various Campus Settings

As mentioned earlier in this book, one of the exciting aspects of Covenant Discipleship groups on campus is the variety of settings which can be used successfully.

CHURCH, CHAPEL, OR CAMPUS RELIGIOUS CENTER

Obviously, one of the most often used settings would be a small meeting room in a church or campus chapel. Arrangements can be made very easily with the office manager, and this setting provides a high degree of intimacy with a minimum of distractions and interruptions.

This setting is also convenient for "piggy-backing" a Covenant Discipleship group meeting with another regularly scheduled meeting at the same location. Students often prefer to have two events over one block of time rather than to come out twice during the week for separate meetings. A Covenant Discipleship group might meet immediately before a regularly scheduled student weekly luncheon or dinner, for instance. Having both events in the same location, linking in time, is something that the students can appreciate as a good opportunity for effective time management.

DORMITORIES

A group of students in the same or adjoining dormitories might find it convenient to meet in a dormitory room or study lounge. This often provides a good degree of privacy and intimacy, and experience shows that non-United Methodist students who are invited to a Covenant Discipleship group may feel more comfortable attending a group meeting outside the church building itself. The dormitory is good "middle ground" for such people.

Lisa Ladendorff, who has led a Covenant Discipleship group in the Yuma Residence Hall at the University of Arizona, said, "The dormitory is a comfortable meeting place and very convenient for those of us who live there. It keeps us from having to spend a half hour going to another place to meet."

STUDENT APARTMENTS

Evening meetings may be most convenient for students who are both employed and attending classes during the day. Such a group may be small, but there may not be another setting available at the time they can meet. Don't assume that a group of three or four persons will make the Covenant Discipleship group experience inferior to one in a group of seven; the opposite may be the case. Some students who have been members of a group of three or four members indicate that they had extremely positive experiences in a group of that size. Some of these people have also been members of larger groups at other times and indicate that each group size has its own advantages. Kelly Lawrence, a student Covenant Discipleship group leader at the University of Arizona, said, "I've been in three different Covenant Discipleship groups, two of which had six members and one which had four members. While the larger groups gave more variety of input, I found the smaller group to be the most dynamic, as it was easier to find common spiritual ground and to choose covenant clauses we were all deeply interested in working on."

A student's apartment is not the ideal place for a Covenant Discipleship group meeting. "I'd definitely take the phone off the hook as a first step," said Stacey Kidman, who has led a Covenant Discipleship group in a student apartment at the University of Arizona. "Also, if others live in the apartment, it would be good for the group to meet at a time when only group members are present," said Kidman.

The advantage to using an apartment is that it may be the only available meeting place for some students. In addition, Kidman said, "it is nice to be able to sit in the middle of the living room floor with your shoes off."

STUDENT UNION BUILDING

The student union building offers yet another possible location on campus for a Covenant Discipleship group. Because college covenant groups meet only while classes are in session, the union would usually be accessible to students at the time they want to meet.

For privacy, it may be desirable to schedule a private room in the union building for the weekly meeting. This could be done at a mealtime or at another time covenient to group members.

If the student union provides a central location, and no private rooms are available, a quiet corner of the general dining area might work very well. Experience suggests that college students have a greater ability to block out surrounding noise than most people. With the meeting agenda and focus already set, it is not impossible for a college Covenant Discipleship group to meet in a public place. An open area may not be the most desirable setting, but it may be the only way some students are able to participate. This is especially true for the community college campus.

CAMPUS COFFEE SHOP

One would not think that a restaurant or coffee shop would provide either the intimacy or privacy needed for a Covenant Discipleship group. Still, when the group meets at 7:00 A.M. on Tuesdays, as does the group led by Peter Booth at the University of Arizona, the coffee shop is not always busy and it is not easy to find another location that would serve any better.

Booth said of the Covenant Discipleship group that meets at Mike's Place, "It has pluses and minuses. It is a natural meeting place and it is a good informal setting for breaking the ice as the group is getting started. Eating together and sharing coffee gives a positive feeling to the group. On the other hand, if there are neighbors around you, some group members may lower their voices when they come to a certain point in reporting about the covenant. So you're aware of other people around you when the place is busy."

Regular attendance and commitment have not suffered because of the setting at the coffee shop. In fact, the breakfast group has taken on a bold outreach program with the community food bank in Tucson as one of the acts of compassion in their covenant.

SUMMARY

What does all this mean in terms of the setting for a college Covenant Discipleship group?

Alternative settings are not intended to be used in an effort to be trendy or faddish. They are used only when they are the only reasonable alternative for certain groups of students. When necessary, alternative settings appear to work for college Covenant Discipleship groups. College students, more than most groups, seem to be adaptable and flexible to various surroundings.

The ideal setting for a Covenant Discipleship group, to be sure, is a private room in a church or campus center. When this is possible and convenient to all group members, it is preferred. The selection of a location for a college Covenant Discipleship group, however, may have more to do with student schedules and convenient centralized locations on campus than in other settings. In terms of ecumenicity and campus evangelism—both by-products of the Convenant Discipleship program—a nonchurch setting is often less threatening to students who are of different dominations or who may be wary of church groups on campus because of their experiences.

The rule of thumb should be to allow students to try out a location and setting, with evaluation to follow in four to six weeks. If participation would be impossible in the more traditional settings and times, it is certainly worth the chance. Experience suggests that in college groups, flexibility and adaptation are possible without any major adverse effect on the program.

XI. Evaluation

In the Covenants on Campus program, an annual end-of-the-year evaluation should be done two or three weeks before students are faced with final examinations. Because group members have been involved by this time for almost an entire school year, they are able to give helpful feedback concerning their own experience with the Covenant Discipleship program.

Two methods of evaluation prove to be valuable. The first is a group evaluation session. If more than one Covenant Discipleship group is active, this is a chance to get all participants and group leaders together with the campus minister or Covenant Discipleship program director.

THE GROUP EVALUATION SESSION

Helpful questions for group evaluation might include the following, among others which are specific to the local situation:

1. What did you find most helpful about the Covenant Discipleship program this year to your life as a student and as a Christian?

2. Are there specific things we can work to improve as we plan the program for next year? What would help the Covenant Discipleship groups to work better on our campus?

3. How can we effectively tell other students about the benefits of involvement in Covenant Discipleship groups and invite new people to become participants in next year's program?

The group evaluation session might become a special event such as a pizza dinner or dessert supper. It is important to provide students with a special incentive for attending, especially at this time of the year. As final examinations approach, "evaluation session" might not only sound boring, but it might even seem to be questionable stewardship of time. Still, this is the time of year when responses are fresh and best formulated in students' minds. The information gained is most helpful to the director and group leaders; therefore, special preparation should be done to make the invitation to the group evaluation session exciting and to make the actual evaluation session worthwhile.

THE INDIVIDUAL EVALUATION FORMS

A second, individual opportunity for group members to offer evaluation does not prove redundant. Individual evaluation forms, sent to each Covenant Discipleship group member with a self-addressed, stamped return envelope, will provide another opportunity for honest feedback concerning the program. The opportunity should be provided for these evaluations to be anonymous, although students may have the option to sign them.

Students who may hesitate to speak up in the group evaluation session have an opportunity to reflect on their experiences and take time to answer on the written form. This format seems to be most inviting for honest criticism. A mature leader, like any human being, might become somewhat defensive concerning critical remarks about a Covenant Discipleship program. Spending time with the written questionnaires, however, will prove helpful to the leader as groups are planned for ensuing years. A mature leader will, over the course of time, be able to evaluate which critical remarks are valid and which may not be constructive.

Some questions that might be included on the individual evaluation form are:

1. What was the most important personal benefit you received from your participation in a Covenant Discipleship group this year?

2. As we look toward next year, how can we improve the Covenant Discipleship group experience for students? List specific things you think could be improved, and offer any suggestions you may have in those areas.

3. When we look for students to lead a Covenant Discipleship group, we look for someone who allows others to have their own opinions, who can lead the group process effectively, and is dedicated to working on her or his Christian discipleship. Was there a member of your group you would recommend to be a Covenant Discipleship group leader in the future?

Annual evaluation is essential to a successful college Covenant Discipleship program. It allows students to voice any concerns they may have, and the information received by the leader provides helpful guidance and direction for the future.

XII. Renewing the Covenants

Ational research data indicate that the renewal of the covenant and continuing Covenant Discipleship groups from term to term are among the most difficult tasks facing the Covenants on Campus program. Many groups have yet to decide the best procedure for this. Others have chosen to handle the situation in one of a variety of ways but report that there are benefits and drawbacks to each method.

In local churches, where it is understood that a Covenant Discipleship group might remain together for many years, the continuity helps the members get to know each other. As the group grows in discipleship from year to year, the challenges to each member increase, especially as the trust level between group members increases. This is not possible, by nature, with college Covenant Discipleship groups. Scheduling conflicts from term to term, changes in personal schedules from year to year, and graduation and transience among the members of college groups produce increased challenges.

Therefore, special effort must be made to accept these limitations and to look for alternative strengths that may be possible in the college and university setting. Fortunately, as previously mentioned, students are highly adaptable and able to adjust to necessary changes.

One of the goals of college Covenant Discipleship groups is that participants will go on in the life of the church after their graduation to begin new Covenant Discipleship groups in churches all over the country, using the traditional model outlined in *Covenant Discipleship: Christian Formation Through Mutual Accountability* by David Lowes Watson.

This has begun to happen. Four recent graduates of the University of Arizona—Nick and Lisa Clay Strobel, Gwen Sweeney, and Noma Ladendorff—are all now living in Seattle, Washington. All were members of a Covenant Discipleship group in Tucson and intend to begin a Covenant Discipleship group in their new church home in Seattle. The Section on Covenant Discipleship in Nashville would like to hear of similar stories from throughout the country as students carry the Covenant Discipleship program into local churches.

A second goal is the development of church leadership among college students, the largest segment of individuals by age group to become inactive church members. Each member of a Covenant Discipleship group is exposed to a leadership role as she or he takes a regular turn at leading the group throughout the year. Those with special gifts are identified by the director or leader for further development of their leadership skills as a Covenant Discipleship group leader. This by-product of the program is not insignificant in the college setting where future church leadership is being formed.

THE TIME FOR RENEWING GROUPS

The predominant method used throughout the country for renewing covenant groups is to keep the college Covenant Discipleship group members together throughout a full academic year. If a group is having a valuable experience together after the first term, then, quite possibly, they will make a strong effort to find a meeting time during the second term where all can continue to participate in that same group together.

My own experience with eight different groups is that 95 percent of all participants have expressed a strong preference that the group should stay together for at least one full academic year. In the ensuing year, some members of that group might be committed to remaining together and can do so as new groups are scheduled. The beginning of the new academic year also seems to be the time when college Covenant Discipleship groups seem ready to split into two cells and reach out to include new people into each group. Students seem to feel that developing a covenant during the first term consumes a great deal of time and energy, and to repeat the process during the second term seems to be time better spent by continuing in a group where the covenant has been set.

I strongly suggest keeping college Covenant Discipleship groups together for a complete academic year whenever possible. Keeping groups together from year to year may not be possible, but the opportunity should be offered.

However, it might be necessary in some settings to change groups every academic term. This is done on several campuses, with mixed reviews. Richard Coldwell of Ohio Northern University said, "This is the most awkward part of campus Covenant Discipleship groups." Other campus ministers frequently mention that though some members drop out from term to term, recruiting new members has not been a problem. There is a sense of loss reported, however, when students who must drop out find no new group with which to meet.

The ideal answer to this situation is to vigorously recruit possible student leaders and give those student leaders training (see Appendix B) as well as authority to lead a Covenant Discipleship group, which can incorporate participants with scheduling problems who wish to continue. It has been proven without question that students can handle the responsibility of Covenant Discipleship group leadership; after the pilot group meets for a year, the campus minister does not need to be the Lone Ranger of leadership in the program.

A second approach is to meet at a time that is available to all. At our university, this means meeting at 7:00 A.M., before 8:00 classes. Though I had reservations about that time slot when beginning two years ago, all the 7:00 A.M. groups we have developed—one each term for two years—have been full with seven members.

WORKING NEW MEMBERS INTO THE GROUP

All the possibilities for a Covenant Discipleship group becoming a clique seem to be present. However, our experience is that new members have seemed to feel very welcome when joining an existing group.

After the initial group has developed a covenant and a new member wishes to join, at least two possibilities exist. One possibility is that the group can ask the new member to read the covenant and see if he or she can accept this existing covenant.

This is a good idea. The new member will learn much about the program and about his or her compatibility with the goals of this particular group by reading their covenant.

If the new member agrees to the covenant, he or she can be accepted into the group. Any group, of course, can adjust the covenant at any time by adding, deleting, or adjusting clauses. When a new member joins, it might provide a good opportunity to discuss the covenant and to add new challenges if it seems appropriate. The personal open clauses are always available to the new member, as well.

The second possibility is that when a new member joins, the Covenant Discipleship group can intentionally rewrite the group covenant or revise it significantly. It takes several weeks to do this, of course, and with the limited number of meetings during an academic year, a campus Covenant Discipleship group may not want to consider this. However, this option has the benefit of integrating the new member fully into the group. If two or three members join the group, this option becomes much more attractive and important.

STARTING NEW GROUPS: A CASE STUDY

On campus, starting new Covenant Discipleship groups is necessary to the life of the program. We have discussed the importance of developing student leadership to make this possible. We have also pointed out the need for flexibility in times and locations on campus so that Covenant Discipleship groups become a realistic possibility for the greatest possible number of students.

At the University of Arizona, a pilot group was formed the first semester we started the Covenant Discipleship program. When we returned to campus for the second semester, twenty-two students indicated they wished to be a part of a Covenant Discipleship group. We started three new groups that second semester for a total of four groups on campus. One group was led by a student, Lisa Clay, who had attended a national training seminar for Covenant Discipleship groups. The other three groups were led by the campus minister who had attended the same seminar.

From these four Covenant Discipleship groups, I identified several possible Covenant Discipleship group leaders. I wrote a personal letter to each asking whether he or she would serve as a leader in the fall semester, with the understanding there would be leadership development training sessions for them. Six of the eight students accepted. One of the others agreed to be available if there was need, though it would have presented scheduling problems with her employment.

One month before fall semester began, I set the date for the leadership training as the first Saturday morning of the semester and wrote another personal letter to each student leader. The agenda for that meeting included the paper in Appendix B, with time for questions. Because all had been through at least one semester of participation, the training session was not difficult. We then decided when and where the student leaders wished to offer groups during the week. The variety included one Monday group in a dormitory at 6:15 P.M.; two Wednesday groups at 4:45 P.M. immediately preceding our Wesley Foundation Wednesday night student dinner at 6:00 P.M.; one Thursday 7:00 A.M. group at a coffee shop adjacent to campus; a Friday evening (6:30 P.M.) group at a student apartment off campus; and a Sunday noon group. All six meetings have worked well. Thirty-six students are participating weekly.

A seventh group is being started, which will be led by the campus minister and will be open to ecumenical membership at the Campus Christian Center, which houses eight Protestant denominations.

Throughout the year, the student Covenant Discipleship group leaders meet regularly with the campus minister for mutual support, reporting, and consultation. During this time, the student leaders are also suggesting possible future Covenant Discipleship group leaders they have identified in their groups. I will get to know these prospective leaders and will write to them in the spring, following the same leadership development procedures from year to year. The number of groups offered each year is determined by the number of student leaders available.

Recruitment was done primarily by printed brochures, an information session, and word of mouth. Of these, word of mouth and personal invitation were responsible for 90 percent of the students participating in Covenant Discipleship groups in the second year of the program. Informational brochures explaining the

Covenant Discipleship group program were sent to the entire student mailing list over the summer, announcing a general information session without further obligation during the first week of the fall semester.

This information session included a review of the paper found in Appendix B, along with a sample Covenant Discipleship group meeting and a question-and-answer period. Though students attended the information session without obligation, we announced that at the end of the meeting, during refreshments, lists of group leaders and Covenant Discipleship group times would be posted on newsprint sheets around the room. These newsprint sheets listed the times and locations decided by the student leaders at the leadership training meeting earlier. An extra sheet was available for students who were interested in the program but were unable to attend at any of the offered times.

The general process outlined above has worked very well. However, we have made some important discoveries.

In the first year, the pilot group should remain together. The members of our initial pilot group felt somewhat cheated when the group split to start three new groups at the beginning of second semester to meet student requests.

Should I have it all to do over, the pilot group would remain together and individual members would go out to the new groups for a few weeks to assist them in the development of their group covenant. However, this would be with the understanding that the pilot group member was not a member of the new group; he or she would be "on loan" to assist with the writing of the covenant. When the covenant is completed, group members can easily take responsibility for the meetings. The pilot group member could then return to the pilot group.

Second, an individual should not attempt to be part of—much less lead—more than one Covenant Discipleship group at a time. I was thrilled at the interest of twenty-two students at the beginning of second semester that first year. Because I had not developed enough student leadership at that point, I decided to lead three of the groups myself. As a result, I was not fully a part of any one group and was not able to be fair to any one of them as a leader. Again, a solution would be to meet with the new group to help it develop the group covenant and learn how to proceed with a weekly Covenant Discipleship group meeting, then leave the group on its own. Every new group has indicated that it is quite capable of doing this, once the covenant is completed.

DEVELOPING COVENANT GROUPS ON CAMPUS

A SUGGESTED TIME OUTLINE

1. FIRST YEAR, FALL
Development of a pilot Covenant Discipleship group to meet for one year.

2. FIRST YEAR, SPRING
Personal contact with prospective student leaders to lead groups in the fall.

3. SECOND YEAR, FALL
Leadership training session to begin first semester (letter to prospective leaders one month prior). Use "Covenant Discipleship Group" (Appendix B). Allow time for questions and answers. List times and locations on newsprint sheets.

4. SECOND YEAR, FALL
Introductory information session for student recruits. Use "Covenant Discipleship Group" (Appendix B). Roleplay a sample Covenant Discipleship group meeting briefly. Serve refreshments as students sign up on newsprint for dates and times.

5. SECOND YEAR, WINTER   Offer one new Covenant Disciple-
                         ship group, led by the campus
                         minister.

Repeat the process, #2-5, each academic year.

XIII. The College Covenant Discipleship Group and the Local Church

Kenda Creasy Dean

Of all the messages communicated to the student by a college Covenant Discipleship group, the most important one is "Just do it." Don't agonize over the limits of serving your neighbor; don't get bogged down in the inadequacies of your prayer life or the simplicity of your worship. Just do it. That is the message.

Not every spiritual couch potato on campus is ready for a Covenant Discipleship group, just as not everyone who needs to lose weight can handle an aerobics class. Just as the muscle grows stronger, more flexible, and more efficient with the discipline of exercise, so discipleship grows more surefooted, more productive, and more rewarding as the discipline we have agreed to live out in our covenants is exercised.

COVENANT DISCIPLESHIP
AND THE COLLEGE STUDENT

The purpose of Covenant Discipleship groups is Christian accountability, and there is good reason to support their proliferation on campus. While corporate discipleship is a way of life that will continue long after the young adult years, experiencing challenging Christian commitment as a young adult is particularly powerful. No one is more ripe for commitment than the young adult, and no form of spirituality meets the developmental needs of young adults as neatly as corporate discipleship.

In the first place, corporate discipleship (such as Covenant Discipleship groups) offers students a supportive and intimate place to test new understandings of their identity. Because the purpose of covenant discipleship is the transformation of the person—"to watch over one another in love, that they might help each other to work out their salvation"—the college Covenant Discipleship member (who is continuing her adolescent search for identity through her mid-twenties, anyway) now involves Christ in her self-definition. Her Covenant Discipleship group is one of the few groups she will join that will overtly ask of her certain behaviors and will shape her in a specific direction on purpose. She will emerge from her covenant group each week knowing that discipleship is not a matter of what you *do*. It is a matter of *whose you are*. Her identity is unique because it is not a matter of *who*, but of *whose*.

A second reason the Covenant Discipleship group experience is especially powerful for college students has to do with the corporate form of this means of grace. If establishing identity is the ascendent developmental need of late adolescence, establishing intimacy is the crowning development task of early adulthood. The supportive and intimate environment of the small group is nearly always compelling to young adults. Add to that a group of people who risk together—who consciously form a bond based on a faith that runs counter to the dominant college culture—and the significance of the group for character formation work is apparent.

COVENANT DISCIPLESHIP AND THE LOCAL CHURCH

Ecclesiolae in Ecclesia

The class meeting began when Wesley borrowed from the Moravians the idea of *ecclesiolae in ecclesia*—little churches within the big church. Like the base communities that intensify the witness of the church in Latin America, the class meeting—or today, the Covenant Discipleship group—intensifies the witness of the church on campus by overtly acting out Christ's call for piety and mercy. These "little churches" are reminders of why Christ called the "big church" into being.

Little churches cannot function authentically, however, if separated from the big church. David Lowes Watson explains in *The Early Methodist Class Meeting:*

> If the ecclesiola breaks with the ecclesia, then it becomes detraditioned and vulnerable to the exigencies of its context. Contemporary examples are not difficult to find: a self-centered piety masquerades as true religion . . .

political liberations which meet the criteria of biblical justice in all but the most crucial—obedience to the Godhead revealed in Jesus Christ.[35]

The realization that the "little church" must remain within the "big church" is important for American campus ministry. Often in the past twenty years, campus ministry groups have been distanced from local congregations. Also, while conservative parachurch organizations aggressively proselytized (and flourished) in the 1970s, they did little to encourage students to form long-term relationships with worshiping congregations.

On the other end of the spectrum, mainline churches—recognizing society's need for ecumenical tolerance and young adults' need for a religious environment that welcomes self-examination and criticism—traded in much denominational (and congregationally based) programming in the 1970s for shared resources and ecumenical alternatives. The *modus operandi* for many campus ministry units became the ministry of presence, a strategy that avoided proselytizing and de-emphasized denominational identity in favor of broadly cooperative interfaith projects.

While these strategies created ecumenical tolerance, many did little to promote real understanding of individual faith traditions precisely because the design tended to separate students from the place where these traditions are celebrated and observed: the local church. Today, campus ministers are seeing a different situation. Many students today are wary of local congregations and find the ecumenical campus ministry a supportive and nonthreatening entry point into the life of faith. However, many other students entering college today come from positive local church experiences and have already found meaning in the Christian identity that has begun to be shaped in them through a specific religious tradition. Students who want to deepen their spiritual identity and want a supportive community of faith find only part of what they need in an ecumenical model of the type that is separated from the local church. The part that is missing in such cases is the church—a specific congregation of believers who consciously act out a denominational tradition to establish who they are in the multicultural, multiflavored family of God.

COLLEGE COVENANT DISCIPLESHIP GROUPS
Sinews of the Church

Wesley described the members of the class as the "sinews" of the church. They were muscles that strengthened the church and, though seldom obvious in and of themselves, connected and mobilized the Body of Christ to accomplish the work of God. The relationship of the college Covenant Discipleship group and a local church works much the same way. These students, like covenant discipleship members of all ages, are serious about their church involvement and develop leadership skills within a congregation because they have covenanted to exercise these skills regularly. Their constancy provides "sinews" in the Body of Christ that mobilize the joints and limbs near them, including those in the congregation where they worship.

Yet one factor alone creates a distinct difference between college Covenant Discipleship groups and other forms of corporate discipleship: transience. Membership in Covenant Discipleship is predicated on one's commitment to make corporate discipleship a *way of life.* Yet each semester brings radical changes in student schedules; each summer brings geographic upheaval; and (if by sheer grace a student survives all this) there is still graduation to contend with. Of course, "Pomp and Circumstance" begs the obvious question: Once a student leaves his or her campus Covenant Discipleship group, then what?

The answer lies in the local church. Even though many campus ministry programs are technically independent of any one local congregation, the mooring for corporate discipleship is found, above all, in the worshiping community. The local church and campus ministry unit alike must recognize the college student's need to continue his or her discipleship beyond the college years in the nurturing context of community. We tend to expect youth who have had a positive youth group experience in a local church to automatically become lively participants in a campus church when they leave home for college. Those of us in campus ministry know that this does not automatically happen. It happens *if* the student discovers the same meaningful relationships in the campus church that he or she had in the home congregation.

By the same token, the committed college senior, upon arriving in a new community to work, does not automatically flex the muscle of discipleship in the new environment. Jesus called the twelve disciples for a reason: The whole premise of corporate discipleship is that Christian discipleship requires companionship for the journey. And if a committed college senior, who has grown in faith through Covenant Discipleship during four years at college, finds no intentionally supportive group for discipleship in the new location, then that graduate's obedience to Christ can be in jeopardy.

For these reasons, the relationship between the college Covenant Discipleship group and the local church is both interdependent and selfless. One cannot exist without the other. The church without corporate discipleship risks empty formality and isolationism. The Covenant Discipleship group without the larger church risks purposelessness and acculturation. At the same time, no one campus ministry organization or congregation is the location of covenant discipleship. Covenant Discipleship is about accountability as we act out what we worship. There comes a time when acting out the story of Christ means leaving Nazareth for Jerusalem in order to live out God's call outside the educational womb.

Campus ministry organizations, as well as congregations located near colleges, realize that they serve as training camps for young athletes who will run their Olympic races elsewhere. Unlike the traditional Covenant Discipleship groups, which tend to foster leadership in the host congregation, the discipleship sinews strengthened by grace through a college Covenant Discipleship group probably will have relatively little impact on the church the student attends while in school. College Covenant Discipleship is an investment in the church universal. The permanent location of these students' Christian commitment has yet to be discovered. Their discipleship "muscle" will most likely be felt elsewhere, in some yet-to-be-discovered congregation in that yet-to-be-tried "real world."

HOW CAMPUS MINISTRY UNITS CAN WORK
WITH LOCAL CHURCHES

The benefits of Covenant Discipleship are not limited to the university chapel. One of the most important ways local churches can support Covenant Discipleship on campus is to inaugurate Covenant Discipleship within the congregation. Not only does this underscore the significance of conscious discipleship for all members, including college students, but it offers the ongoing support of corporate discipleship to students home for the summer, or for young adults coming out of a strong campus ministry experience and who need the continued nurture of a group to hold them accountable for their Christian witness.

Another powerful form of support is for the local church to expose students to accountable discipleship before they enter college. *Branch groups,* a high school form of Covenant Discipleship, offer a challenging form of discipleship early in the process of identity-formation, which increases the chance that a student will seek out the support of a Covenant Discipleship group once that student continues the quest for identity away from home. Branch groups also model a "limited contract" version of Covenant Discipleship, a form of limited time commitment recommended in Chapter 12 of this book for college groups, as well.

A third way the local church may support college Covenant Discipleship groups is by sponsoring college chaplains to attend Covenant Discipleship training events. Once exposed to the concept of Covenant Discipleship, most campus ministers immediately recognize its value and practicality in the college environment. After all, Wesley first experimented with corporate discipleship when he was a college student at Oxford. But in general, corporate discipleship is a lost art among Protestants. Steeped in personal religiosity and American individualism, we tend to confuse the mission of the church (what we *do* toward one another) with the purpose of the church (union with God). This is fatal, programmatically and theologically. We forget that discipleship is the work of the community. Only by incorporating the "General Rules of Discipleship" will campus ministry, once again, become the church.

Congregations that are physically near a college campus may support Covenant Discipleship in more specific ways. If Covenant Discipleship is already in place on campus, these churches will conceivably feel the impact through increased student interest in worship and perhaps programs (though not necessarily "college-age" programs). If a Covenant Discipleship group is not in place on campus, then the local church's opportunity is clear: Work with your campus minister to start one.

The local church may work with campus ministers to initiate Covenant Discipleship on campus in a number of ways. We have found it successful to offer groups that involve both congregational members and students (these meet at the church and tend to attract graduate students), as well as groups that involve only undergraduates along with a campus chaplain and the pastor of a local church (these meet in the ecumenical campus chapel and have the additional benefit of demonstrating cooperation between United Campus Ministries and area congregations). Still another congregational initiative involves laypersons who have been through a Covenant Discipleship group experience themselves and who work with campus ministers to convene satellite student groups, which meet in dorms, the library, or some other public space. (NOTE: Universities have varying policies about allowing non-university personnel on campus. Be sure to obtain the appropriate permission ahead of time, or you will be in violation of trespassing laws. This is another instance in which working with the campus minister is obviously beneficial.)

CONCLUSION

The relationship between the college Covenant Discipleship group and the local church will always stand in some tension, yet one cannot exist without the other. The *ecclesiola* witnesses to the church and to the community; the *ecclesia* is God's promised witness to us. The "little church" is not in competition with the "big church"; college Covenant Discipleship augments and strengthens the local church, while the local congregation can provide support as well as an environment for faithful questioning in which many forms of discipleship can flourish. The question is not *how* you are a disciple, but *that* you are. Just do it, and leave the rest to God.

Appendix A: Checklist for the Weekly Covenant Discipleship Group Leader

THE FORM OF A COVENANT DISCIPLESHIP GROUP MEETING

Author's Note: After the covenant is developed and signed, student leaders take turns leading the weekly meeting of the group. This form may be used as a guideline for use by the student leader for the weekly Covenant Discipleship group meeting.

_____ 1. Opening prayer
_____ 2. Proceed immediately to the covenant.
    A. Each clause is taken in order.
    B. Beginning with self, the leader asks each member whether the intent expressed in the clause has been fulfilled during the week.
    C. All respond, then the leader directs the attention of the group to the next clause.
_____ 3. Personal open clauses from the previous week (if any) are accepted.
_____ 4. Closing prayers and concerns (prayers for others).
_____ 5. Housekeeping matters for the following week
    A. Who will lead?
    B. Where will the meeting be held? When?
    C. Who will contact the absentees?

BASIC RESPONSIBILITIES OF THE WEEKLY GROUP LEADER

The group leader for the week sets the example for the other members of the group and must be especially diligent in communicating to all group members that accountability does not mean inflicting guilt on, scolding, lecturing, or criticizing others. It may mean to refrain from giving unwanted advice. At no time should hurtful, insensitive words be tolerated. The group leader bears the major responsibility for making sure that the group operates with an attitude of respect and common courtesy.

Appendix B:
Covenant Discipleship Group

Author's Note: This Appendix may be used in at least two ways. It can be used as a general introduction for students who are unfamiliar with the Covenant Discipleship group program and who may want to consider taking part. This can be done at an introductory session such as the one outlined in Chapter 9. It can also be used as the outline for a leadership training session with prospective student Covenant Discipleship group leaders, as suggested in Chapter 9.

Many university students learn that living out their Christian faith publicly on campus is very challenging. These students sense that there is little sympathy for their religious values and for their desire to live out the faith. David Lowes Watson suggests, correctly, that this dilemma is not limited to the college campus: "It has always been difficult to sustain a faithful Christian witness in the world, because the world is not yet the kingdom of God."[36]
Wesley organized the early Methodist class meetings to help Christian people with this problem.

> The class meeting was a weekly gathering, a subdivision of the early societies, at which members were required to give account to one another of their discipleship and thereby to sustain each other in their witness. These meetings were regarded by Wesley as the "sinews" of the Methodist movement, the means by which members "watched over one another in love."[37]

As individuals meet weekly for discipleship, they learn to follow Jesus' one requirement for discipleship—"Follow me"—the way of trusting obedience. This obedience is not always comfortable. It sometimes requires taking a risk. But those who live the Christian life for any period of time know the meaning of the words of Paul when he said, "I do not understand my own actions. For I do not do what I want, but I do the very thing I hate" (Romans 7:15). In other words, even though we know we are to live in faithful obedience to the ways of Christ, we find that it is not easy to do so in the world. Partially, this is because of our own imperfections. But in addition to this fact, the world in which we live is not always very supportive of our desire to live in the Spirit of Christ. Discipleship is, therefore, very hard work. It can easily become discouraging.

For that reason, we might agree when Watson describes the Christian life in the following way: "There are good works to be done, whether or not we are in the right mood. How do we know this? Because Jesus left us with some very close guidelines: to feed the hungry, clothe the naked, help the sick, and visit the prisons. So let's get on with it. And as we do, we will probably bump into Jesus, who is of course there ahead of us."[38] Covenant Discipleship groups are for those who wish to share this challenge.

THE PATTERN OF WESLEY'S CLASS MEETINGS

Covenant Discipleship groups are patterned after the class meetings of John Wesley in England in the eighteenth century. Wesley encouraged weekly meetings among his Christian sisters and brothers for the purpose of discipleship and faith development. "To declare publicly that the commandments of Jesus Christ for personal and social behavior were to be taken seriously, and to pattern their lives accordingly, meant considerable tension in the world in which they lived. It meant 'fighting the good fight of faith' in territory that was by no means neutral;—and they certainly could not wage this fight alone."[39]

Though the idea originated with Wesley, it quickly became apparent that he could not personally lead each group. Lay leadership was a part of this movement from the very beginning. Covenant Discipleship groups also develop lay leadership as the members participate in weekly meetings. Though this is not the primary purpose of the Covenant Discipleship group, it is an important by-product.

Wesley looked for a certain type of person to become a class leader. Primary among requirements was what he called a combination of disciplinary and spiritual discernment. By this, he meant that the individual had to be intentionally leading a life in which he or she was being led by the spirit of God in daily actions.

The class leader was important in many respects. She or he was the initial point of contact with new members. The leader was responsible for the record of attendance at class meetings and for follow-up with absentee members. The class leader also assessed the stage of faith development of each member of the group. Although there was not a qualitative significance attached to one stage above another, the stages of Christian growth leaders were to look for were these:

- "Awakened" (searching for faith)
- "Justified" (new birth in Christ)
- "Gone on to perfection" (mature in the faith)

THE COVENANT

The first task of the Covenant Discipleship group is to write the covenant the group will use in its weekly meetings. This process may take several weeks, and it is not to be hurried. As the covenant is being written, group members begin to learn about each other and appreciate each other. The normal process of writing the covenant includes the following stages:

1. Brainstorm on clauses that should be in the covenant. Allow all members to mention things they think are important. This can usually be done in the first and second one-hour meetings.

2. Copies of all the ideas from the brainstorming session should be in the hands of each group member at the beginning of the second session, if not before. During the second session, group members begin to evaluate the clauses that were listed during the brainstorming session. Some may be removed from further consideration. Other important items may be added at this time. Clauses that are close to each other in content or purpose may be combined. This stage will usually take two to four weeks, depending upon the group.

3. For a clause to be included in the group covenant, all members must agree on it. (Other provisions are made for

individual clauses, as you will see below.) If any member objects to a certain clause, that person should not be pressured to accept it, and it should be dropped. Because Covenant Discipleship group meetings are no longer than one hour, the number of clauses included in the covenant should not number more than ten. This may require further combining or possibly choosing the top ten priority clauses.

THE PARTS OF THE COVENANT

Preamble and Conclusion

The preamble and conclusion of the covenant are "personalizing marks" that allow group members to work out language that describes their purpose for meeting together and their openness to work in accordance with the promptings of the Holy Spirit. The preamble and conclusion should not be lengthy. The preamble should serve as an introduction to the clauses of the covenant, and the conclusion should serve as a summary of the group's purpose in meeting weekly.

Required Clauses

Wesley said that the means of grace are the building blocks for faith development. Taken from the "General Rules for the United Societies," certain clauses are required as the building blocks of a covenant. Required clauses in each covenant must include what Watson calls "The New General Rule of Discipleship: To witness to Jesus Christ in the world, and to follow his teachings through acts of compassion, justice, worship, and devotion, under the guidance of the Holy Spirit."[40]

THE GENERAL RULE OF DISCIPLESHIP

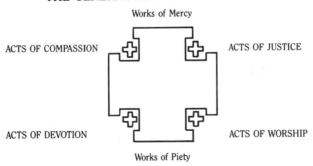

Works of Mercy

ACTS OF COMPASSION   ACTS OF JUSTICE

ACTS OF DEVOTION   ACTS OF WORSHIP

Works of Piety

Therefore, each covenant must include clauses that specifically address the General Rule of Discipleship:

1. Acts of worship
2. Acts of devotion
3. Acts of compassion
4. Acts of justice

As the group goes through the process of developing its covenant, it is a good idea to look at this list often to make sure all the required clauses are represented in the covenant. The way the clause is worked into the covenant is up to the individual group.

Optional, Contextual Clauses

Once the required clauses have been represented, other clauses may be added to the covenant. Contextual clauses are those the entire group has agreed upon as important to corporate discipleship.

Open Clauses

Some members of the group might have a desire to work on some aspect of their discipleship, but other group members may not agree to include that particular clause as a part of the group covenant. When this happens, the individual makes a personal covenant with the group by sharing his or her "open clause" and then being accountable to the group at the following week's meeting.

Things to Remember When Writing the Covenant

Because the length of the weekly meeting is to be no more than one hour, remember to limit the number of clauses in the covenant to ten or fewer. Do not be too general. Each clause should be limited in scope and specific in expectations. Specifics will allow group members to focus more on what they intend to do and will allow them to answer more clearly when the clauses are discussed.

When the covenant has been completed, a final copy is made for each group member. All copies of the covenant are passed around and signed by each of the other members.

Appendix C:
An Ecumenical Invitation to
the Campus

Author's Note: This Appendix may be used to encourage ecumenical participation in the Covenants on Campus program. Simply use Appendix C as a preface and follow with the full contents of Appendix B.

In the context of the college or university campus, Covenant Discipleship groups provide an opportunity for students to put their faith to daily and practical use. Many students discover that it is very challenging to live out their Christian faith publicly on campus.

Because of this, the various and sometimes subtle differences in our denominational stances may cause us to be a fractured community on campus, unable to make significant Christian witness because we are so separated. Our students do not feel part of the larger Body of Christ, which would be a powerful force on campus. The role of individual denominations is important in terms of our "in-house" needs for identity and expression of belief. But when denominationalism causes a fractured Christian witness in the broader community, it is not serving the Body of Christ. In that task, we need each other. We need to support each other. As John Wesley said, we need to "watch over one another in love."

Covenant Discipleship groups are an effort to serve that need in the United Methodist community, but these groups can easily be adapted to the needs of students from the broader Christian community. I agree with what David Lowes Watson, the creator of the Covenant Discipleship group program, has said: "The discerning Christian therefore quickly comes to realize that discipleship is not so much a constant task as it is to be on constant call. At any time, Jesus may require a particular act of compassion, a particular word of justice, or a particular refusal to act or speak. The disciple must be ready for these instructions, which usually come as promptings of the Holy Spirit."[41] Covenant Discipleship groups are for those who wish to share in that endeavor.

I believe that if the concept of Covenant Discipleship groups were firmly understood, there would be no reason why they could not be broadened beyond Protestantism. It would be my hope that our ecumenical effort at the Covenants on Campus program is the precursor for inclusion of the Roman Catholic community on our campus.

CLASS MEETINGS

The idea of Covenant Discipleship groups comes from class meetings held by Wesley in the eighteenth century. Wesley encouraged weekly meetings among small groups of his Christian sisters and brothers for the purpose of discipleship and faith development.

In the ecumenical setting, the fact that this happened in the Methodist tradition is important only as the basis for the valuable work that has been done by Watson in the creation of the Covenant Discipleship group model, which we will be following. Certainly, other denominations can claim similar meetings throughout their history, and an understanding of such meetings for discipleship and faith development will allow other denominations to appreciate the work that has been done by Watson. The book, *Covenant Discipleship: Christian Formation Through Mutual Accountability,* fully explains the program and is available from Discipleship Resources, P. O. Box 189, Nashville, TN 37202; (615) 340-7284.

Appendix D:
Sample Covenants

Author's Note: The danger in printing sample covenants is that groups will simply want to copy them. I strongly discourage this. Working together on the language of your covenant not only makes it unique, it also provides necessary discussion among the members of the Covenant Discipleship group. Read the covenants to get an idea of form, but then write your group covenant in your own language.

1. University United Methodist Church, College Park, Maryland, Kenda Creasy Dean, Campus Minister

"To be a Christian disciple means sharing in Christ's ongoing work of salvation in the world. The task of discipleship therefore calls for the binding together of those with like mind and purpose, to watch over one another in love. . . ."

Preamble to Our Covenant

- We covenant together to be present each week.
- We will open and close our meetings with prayer—to help us focus our minds and hearts on God rather than on ourselves and our accomplishments.
- We will approach each other with honesty and in a spirit of love. Understanding that our purpose is not to judge each other, we will hopefully feel free to speak honestly—both in terms of our keeping with the covenant as well as our failure to do so.
- As Christ does for us, so will we try, to the best of our ability, to "watch over each other in love."
- We covenant together to offer encouragement to each other to grow in faith.

Our Covenant (drafted October 24, 1988, revised September 20, 1989)

I. Works of Piety

- We covenant together to attend a worship service regularly once in the week.
- We covenant together to thoughtfully read and reflect on scripture (the amount is up to each individual) each day.
- We covenant together to take time out every day to pray—a time of intentional prayer, including prayer for each other.
- We covenant together to close with Communion every other week.

II. Works of Mercy

- We commit ourselves to an ongoing form of service throughout the semester.
- We commit ourselves to speak up rather than remain silent in defense of one or ones being unfairly judged or spoken against.
- We commit ourselves to become more conscious of the ways in which we can be more kind to others (may just be smiling more or saying hello).

Our Group

John Beuerle	Kenda Creasy Dean
Rhonda Horried	J.M. Jardina
Kathleen Kline-Chesson	Valerie Brown
Pam De George	

2. Group led by Noma Ladendorff, a senior at the University of Arizona, Tucson

I love thee, O Lord, my strength. The Lord is my rock, and my fortress, and my deliverer, my God, my rock, in whom I take refuge, my shield, and the horn of my salvation, my stronghold. I call upon the Lord, who is worthy to be praised (Psalm 18:1-3a, RSV).

As Christians, we acknowledge God's unconditional love and acceptance of all [God's] creations. God is alive in us and guides us in our journey of faith. With these things in mind we will support and encourage each other in our efforts to follow God's plan for our lives. We will strive to recognize God as: strength, salvation, love, peace, colors, inspirer, comforter, friend, hope, joy.

In order to more fully develop our relationship with God we covenant to the following:

1. To better relate with others I will strive to be accepting, patient, and nonjudgmental of them, always striving to be a good listener, sensitive to their feelings.

2. I will be patient with myself, remembering that I am one of God's creations and as such deserve time for myself, both physically and spiritually. I will remember to allow time for proper eating, sleeping, exercising, and relaxing.

3. I will remember to be thankful for God's blessings in my life during the bad times as well as the good.

4. I will strive for unconditional love and acceptance of all God's creations.

5. I will make a conscious effort to be prayerfully aware of what is going on around me. I will pray daily, remembering in my prayers to include worldwide and community concerns and the other members of the covenant group.

6. I will read this covenant daily. Additionally, I will read spiritual literature in order to become more sensitive to God's guidance and presence in my life.

Recognizing that there are times when we cannot live up to the standards we have set for ourselves we covenant to support each other in an encouraging and constructive manner.

Noma Ladendorff	Heather Anderson
Tammy Blocker	Chris Ludwig
Christy Haas	Gregory Poling

3. Southern Illinois University, Carbondale. Kenneth L. Wallace, Campus Minister

COVENANT OF DISCIPLESHIP

Knowing that Jesus Christ died that I might have eternal life, I herewith pledge myself to be his disciple, holding nothing back, but yielding all to the gracious initiatives of the Holy Spirit. I faithfully pledge my time, my skills, my resources, and my strength, to search out God's will for me, and to obey.

Daily I will read the covenant to evaluate my compliance with it.

I will pray each day, privately, for my family, friends, and nation.

I will read and study the scriptures each day, while praying for God's guidance.

I will worship each week.

I will pray before meals.

I will heed the warning of God's commandments.

I will serve God and my neighbor.

I will pray for myself and care for my body as a living sacrifice for Jesus Christ.

Seeking the guidance of the Holy Spirit, I will make an effort to sustain, improve, and expand Christ's ministry on earth.

I will present myself to others in a Christ-like manner.

Opening and closing with prayer, I will share in Christian fellowship each week where I will be accountable for my discipleship.

I hereby make my commitment, trusting in the grace of God to work in me that I might have strength to keep this covenant.

Date: _____ Signed: _____

4. Group led by Stacey Kidman, graduate student at the University of Arizona, Tucson

Acknowledging that God is our wisdom, we have developed this covenant to enhance our spiritual lives and to guide our actions in doing [God's] will.

1. We will be more sensitive and open-minded toward others.
2. We will be more tolerant and patient toward others.
3. We will do some action each week to remind some friend or family member that he or she is remembered, cared for, and appreciated.
4. We will become more aware of social situations through attention to the news (newspapers, television, magazines, radio).
5. We will each take action to improve our relationship with our natural environment.
6. We commit ourselves to improving our self-discipline in regards to our obligations.
7. We will take time each day for: prayer, in which we will include our C.D.G.; a devotional, such as the *Upper Room* reading; self-reflection and meditation; and anxiety management techniques.

Trusting in Grace, we pledge to support each other as we leave the confines of comfort in our search for spiritual growth.

Stacey Kidman   Kari Perkins   Jennifer Putz

5. Ohio Northern University, Ada, Ohio. Richard E. Coldwell, Campus Minister

A COVENANT OF DISCIPLESHIP

Knowing that Jesus Christ died that I might have eternal life, I pledge myself to be his disciple, holding nothing back, but yielding all to the gracious initiatives of the Holy Spirit. I faithfully pledge my time, my skills, my resources, and my strength, to search out God's will for me, and to obey.

I will obey the promptings of the Holy Spirit to serve God and my neighbor.

I will heed the warnings of the Holy Spirit not to sin against God and my neighbor.

I will worship each week unless prevented.

I will pray each day conventionally and spontaneously, both alone and with my friends.

I will read and study the Scriptures daily.

I will prayerfully care for my body and care for and be informed about the world in which I live.

I will share in Christian fellowship each week where I will be accountable for my discipleship.

I will not let the sun set on my anger.

I will prayerfully plan my study and/or work time.

I hereby make my commitment, trusting in the grace of God to work in me that I might have strength to keep this covenant.

Date: _____   Signed: _____

6. University of Arizona, Tucson. Kim Hauenstein-Mallet, Campus Minister

COVENANT

Looking to Christ as the example of God for all we do, we covenant to be God's disciples and to "watch over each other in love." We will share in Christian community each week where we will be accountable for our discipleship.

As a part of my discipleship:

1. I will seek to practice the presence of God in my daily life, listening for and following the leading of the Holy Spirit in my faith journey.

2. I will prayerfully care for my body and the world in which I live, seeking to love all life and all of God's creation.

3. I will attempt to see people who are difficult in my life as my teachers and to see people in a nonjudgmental way.

4. I will seek an intentional way to be a considerate friend to my "neighbor."

5. I will pray daily, making time in my life for an intentional relationship with God. My prayers will include intercessions for others, for peace and justice in the world, and for my

university. I will include all the members of my Covenant Discipleship group in my daily prayers.

6. I will read the Scriptures daily and prayerfully consider that I have read.

Trusting in grace, we commit ourselves to follow this Covenant with confidence in God's direction.

Lisa Clay	Kim Hauenstein-Mallet
Kelly Lawrence	Lorraine Hauenstein-Mallet
Susan Ogilvie	Gregory Poling

Appendix E:
Sample Student Recruitment Letter

Author's Note: The following letter can be adapted to be used as an invitation to prospective pilot group members or as an initial recruitment letter for the following year, when new groups are being started. It should be written on your campus ministry or church letterhead, following suggestions made in Chapters 5 and 9.

Date

Dear _____,

This Tuesday morning at 7:00 A.M. we will have an introductory session for Covenant Discipleship groups. We will meet in the conference room of the Campus Christian Center, 715 N. Park Avenue.

Covenant Discipleship group is an outstanding program in which the participants agree to develop a covenant and to meet together weekly for one hour. The covenant includes daily devotions, when members of the group pray for each other and remember each other's joys and struggles. The covenant includes the intention to worship regularly.

Members also agree to be involved in works of mercy toward others; these include works of justice and compassion. At the weekly Covenant Discipleship group meeting, members report to each other about their efforts in Christian discipleship. This is done in an atmosphere of support and encouragement, never judgmentalism or criticism.

We will have a continental breakfast of pastries, juice, and coffee this Tuesday at 7:00, and I will explain how Covenant Discipleship meetings work. Those who decide to take part may then decide on a time for future meetings; those who decide that the program is too demanding for their schedules right now will not be made to feel any further obligation beyond Tuesday.

I hope you can join us Tuesday morning.

Yours in Christ's Spirit,
Kim Hauenstein-Mallet, Campus Minister

Appendix F:
A Form for Daily Prayer

Author's Note: Many times, members of college Covenant Discipleship groups ask for assistance with their efforts at daily devotions. Below is a general form for daily prayer. Other printed resources for daily devotions may be found in Appendix I: Suggested Resources.

A FORM FOR DAILY PRAYER

1. PRAYER
   A personal prayer to seek God's presence, or this:
   Eternal Spirit, whose love is proven in the gift of Jesus Christ, open my eyes and ears and heart to any message you might have for me today. As I read the scriptures and seek their meaning for my life, bless me with the gift of understanding, through the Spirit of Christ. Amen.

2. READING FROM A PSALM

3. DAILY SCRIPTURE READING
   Suggestions (See Appendix I):
   1. *The Upper Room Disciplines*
   2. *A Guide for Prayer*
   3. Read through the New Testament of *The Oxford Annotated Bible* with a reputable biblical commentary to help with interpretation.

4. CLOSING PRAYERS: FOR THE CHURCH, FOR OTHERS, FOR SELF

5. TIME FOR REFLECTION
   Suggestions (See Appendix I):
   1. Devotional Reading
   2. Silent Meditation
   3. Journal Writing

6. THE LORD'S SUPPER

Note: You will never "find" time for daily prayer. Our busy lives must be disciplined to include it and to experience such discipline. We must be convinced of the importance of daily prayer and meditation in our lives; that is, we must hold it as a value. Then the fifteen to thirty minutes a day will seem essential to our spiritual health rather than obligatory or forced. An excellent guide is *Celebration of Discipline* by Richard J. Foster (see Appendix I).

The *Oxford Annotated Bible* is recommended because it includes good maps, articles on the Bible, chapter introductions, and helpful footnotes to each verse.

Appendix G:
Rules, &c. of the United Societies

Author's Note: The General Rules affirm that genuine discipleship is rooted in living out the Christian faith. John Wesley published these in 1743 as a set of guidelines for the Societies as a whole.

Creative efforts could easily incorporate some of the General Rules into a contemporary covenant: do no harm, avoid evil; do good: take care of people's physical needs first, then spiritual needs; attend upon the ordinances of God: the spiritual disciplines are linked to the larger church.

The word Rules might indicate legalism to us. But Wesley's belief was clearly that works are a means of grace. In other words, by doing things, we open ourselves to grace.

1. IN the later End of the Year 1739, eight or ten Persons came to me in London, who appeared to be deeply convinced of Sin, and earnestly groaning for Redemption. They desired (as did two or three more the next Day) that I would spend some Time with them in Prayer, and advise them how to flee from the Wrath to come; which they saw continually hanging over their Heads. That we might have more Time for this great Work, I appointed a Day when they might all come together, which from thenceforward they did every Week, namely on Thursday, in the Evening. To these, and as many more as desired to join with them, (for their Number increased daily) I gave those Advices from Time to Time which I judged most needful for them; and we always concluded our Meeting with Prayer suited to their several Necessities.

2. This was the rise of the UNITED SOCIETY, first in London, and then in other Places. Such a Society is no other than a "Company of Men having the Form, and seeking the Power of Godliness, united in order to pray together, to receive the Word of Exhortation, and to watch over one another in Love, that they may help each other to work out their Salvation."

3. That it may the more easily be discern'd, whether they are indeed working out their own Salvation, each Society is divided into smaller Companies, called Classes, according to their respective Places of abode. There are about twelve Persons in every Class: one of whom is stiled *The Leader.* It is his Business

I. To see each Person in this Class, once a Week at the least; in order To receive what they are willing to give, toward the Relief of the Poor;

To advise, reprove, comfort, or exhort, as Occasion may require.

II. To meet the Minister and the Stewards of the Society once a Week; in order

To pay in to the Stewards what they have receiv'd of their several Classes in the Week preceeding;

To shew their Account of what each Person has contributed; And

To inform the Minister of any that are sick, or of any that walk disorderly, and will not be reproved.

4. There is only one Condition previously required, in those who desire Admission into these Societies, *a Desire to flee from the Wrath to come, to be saved from their Sins:* But, wherever this is really fix'd in the Soul, it will be shewn by its Fruits. It is therefore expected of all who continue therein, that they should continue to evidence their Desire for Salvation, *First,* by Doing no Harm, by avoiding Evil in every kind; especially, that which is most genuinely practised. Such is

The taking of the Name of God in vain;

The profaning of the Day of the Lord, either by doing ordinary Work thereon, or by buying and selling: Drunkenness, *Buying or selling Spirituous Liquors; or drinking them* (unless in the Cases of extreme Necessity:)

Fighting, Quarreling, Brawling; *Going to Law,* Returning Evil for Evil, or Railing for Railing: The *using many Words* in buying or selling.

The *buying or selling uncustomed Goods:*

The *giving or taking Things on Usury:*

Uncharitable or unprofitable Conversation:

Doing to others as we would not they should do unto us:
Doing what we know is not for the Glory of God: As
The *putting on of God or costly Apparel.*
The *taking such Diversions* as cannot be used in the Name of
the Lord Jesus:
The *Singing* those *Songs,* or *Reading* those *Books,* which do
not tend to the Knowledge or Love of God:
Softness, and needless Self-indulgence:
Laying up treasures upon Earth.

5. It is expected of all who continue in these Societies, that
they should continue to evidence their Desire of Salvation,
    Secondly, by doing Good, by being in every kind, merciful
after their Power: as they have Opportunity, doing Good of every
possible sort, and as far as is possible, to all Men:
    To their Bodies, of the Ability which God giveth, by giving
Food to the Hungry, by cloathing the Naked, by visiting or helping
them that are Sick, or in Prison:
    To their Souls, by instructing, *reproving* or exhorting all we
have any intercourse with: Trampling under Foot that Enthusi-
astick Doctrine of Devils, that "we are not to do Good," unless *our
Heart be free to it."*
    By doing Good especially to them that are of the Household of
Faith, or groaning so to be: Employing them preferably to others,
buying one of another, helping each other in Business; and that so
much the more, because the World will love its own, and them
only.
    By all possible *Diligence and Frugality,* that the Gospel be not
blamed:
    By running with Patience the Race that is set before them;
denying themselves, and taking up their Cross daily; submitting
to bear the Reproach of Christ, to be as the Filth and Off-scouring
of the World; and looking that Men should say *all manner of Evil of
them falsely, for their Lord's sake:*

6. It is expected of all who desire to continue in these Societies, that they should continue to evidence their Desire of
Salvation,

Thirdly, by attending upon all the Ordinances of God: Such are

The publick Worship of God;
The Ministry of the Word, either read or expounded;
The Supper of the Lord;
Private Prayer;
Searching the Scriptures; and
Fasting, or Abstinence.

7. These are the General Rules of our Societies; all which we are taught of God to observe, even in his written Word, the only Rule, and the sufficient Rule both of our Faith and Practice: And all these we know his Spirit writes on every truly awaken'd Heart. If there by any among us who observe them not, who habitually break any one of them, let it be made known unto [the class leader] who watches over that Soul, as one that must give Account. I will admonish him of the Error of his Ways: I will bear with him for a Season. But if he then repent not, he hath no more Place among us. We have deliver'd our own souls.

JOHN WESLEY

Feb. 23.   1742-3.

Reproduced from the first edition, 1743.

Appendix H:
Commonly Asked Questions

*Author's Note: The following represent eleven of the most fre-
quently asked questions about the college Covenant Discipleship
group program. If you have questions that are not yet fully
satisfied, get in touch with the authors or those who are national
staff representatives by addressing your questions to the Covenant
Discipleship Section, General Board of Discipleship of The United
Methodist Church, P. O. Box 840, Nashville, TN 37202.*

**1. What can you do about members expressing guilty feelings
about having failed in their covenant commitments?**

As the group grows together, the reaction and supportive
comments and actions toward each other will help all members to
turn guilty feelings into a more positive tone. The leader can help
set this tone. The clauses of the covenant are things the members
have set as goals; had they been doing those things easily prior to
the group meetings, they probably would not have included them
in the covenant. Therefore, they are challenges and have been
recognized as such. Usually, the things that are most challenging
to us provide us with the most trouble as we try to accomplish
them. That is the case with the clauses of the covenant. When
group members begin to perform the clauses of the covenant easily
and without failure, it is time to write new and more challenging
clauses. Group members need to realize that guilt feelings about
missing the mark are not as helpful as more positive feelings about
realizing that on this important goal, the individual is confronting
himself or herself each week with an honest evaluation of progress
on the spiritual path.

**2. What can I do for members of my group who are asking for help
with daily and weekly devotional opportunities?**

Personal materials for devotions may be found in Appendix I,
"Resources." The most affordable for students is an annual devotional published by the Upper Room, *The Upper Room Disciplines.*

In addition, group members might want to gather for a weekly time of devotions and Communion together. Some group members may also choose to meet for a weekly Bible study. These additional opportunities should not be mandatory; the primary meeting for the week is the Covenant Discipleship group meeting. For many students, this will be plenty of a time commitment in their lives. But for those who are interested, a weekly devotional time and an opportunity for Bible study might be very supportive.

3. What can we do about schedule conflicts of students with the weekly Covenant Discipleship group schedule?

In the Covenants on Campus program, scheduling conflicts are the norm rather than the exception. This situation is to be expected. There are creative ways to deal with it. First of all, when a new term starts with new schedules, the existing group might be able to schedule a new time that suits all members. If not, and if the group is large enough, it might split into two new cells and invite new members to participate at times that are convenient to all. The group might meet at a time that is available to all even if it is not convenient, such as 7:00 A.M., before classes begin.

4. What happens when the weekly meeting begins to turn into more of a gossip session than a discipleship group?

It is possible that the weekly leader will not have enough awareness of the process to confront this. For this reason, it necessitates intervention by a group leader who has been in a Covenant Discipleship group for at least a year and has been through a leadership training experience such as the one outlined in Appendix B, "Covenant Discipleship Group." This group leader will need to address the situation in the weekly meeting if the weekly leader allows the group to go off on tangents. It is usually enough to suggest that personal agendas can be dealt with after the meeting and that the time constraint of one hour for the group meeting necessitates a focus on the clauses of the covenant. If some people in the group are particularly difficult, the group leader may need to speak to people individually to clarify the purpose of the group.

5. Does the campus minister or a clergyperson need to lead the group?

No. Students who have been to a national Covenant Discipleship group training event are very able to lead a group. If cost does not allow for this training, the campus minister can provide training opportunities for students through the pilot group and then a training session such as the one found in Appendix B. The student leader should be familiar with the contents of *Covenants on Campus: Covenant Discipleship Groups for College and University Students* and should have his or her own copy, when possible. A student should not simply be placed in a Covenant Discipleship group and asked to lead. But students who have been part of a Covenant Discipleship group for a year and have had leadership training are quite capable of leading groups. When this is the case, it is good for the campus minister or clergyperson to meet with student leaders regularly for guidance and to be available for questions about the Covenants on Campus program.

6. What happens when most of my students are not interested in being a part of a Covenant Discipleship group?

This is to be expected. In local churches, it is considered to be a good sign when 10 to 15 percent of the membership becomes interested in taking on this effort to work at discipleship. It is not for everyone. But there are always students who are interested in doing "something more" in terms of their Christian life. A Covenant Discipleship group consists of two to seven members. Therefore, if you are willing to lead and there is one student desiring this opportunity, you have a pilot Covenant Discipleship group!

7. What if you have people of differing theological positions in the group?

The covenant clauses must be agreed to by each member. The Covenant Discipleship group process in writing the covenant becomes a marvelous opportunity for people of differing theological views to better understand one another's spirituality and thus to *really* "watch over one another in love." The language of the final covenant must be acceptable to all. Therefore, persons with uncompromising theological stances will soon become frustrated at their inability to "control" the process. This is a step toward spiritual growth. As the covenant reaches its final revision stages, the group members realize that they have come to know and appreciate each other as individuals on the faith journey together.

8. Isn't the Covenant Discipleship group elitist?

Any small group can become an elitist group. But that would hardly be good discipleship for people who are being honest about themselves in their faith journey. The signs of elitism that must be kept in mind by the group leader include the following: (1) New members would not be welcome in the group; (2) The covenant becomes sacred and unchangeable as group members change; (3) The group refuses to split into two cells when the number of members in the group has reached eight. Groups must be honestly aware of this danger. If outsiders perceive the Covenant Discipleship group as elitist just because the group meets regularly and has a personalized commitment, perhaps the best solution is to invite those persons to attend a group meeting. They will learn that group members are there because they recognize weaknesses in their discipleship, not superiority.

9. Are visitors allowed at Covenant Discipleship group meetings?

Visitors are welcome to attend a meeting, but if they wish to continue with the group they must decide by their third visit. This should be made clear to the visitor during the first visit to the group.

10. What if a group member brings a very serious problem to the weekly group meeting?

Most likely, group members will not be fully trained in counseling or psychotherapy, and if that is the case, spectacular efforts at counseling should not be made. Group members will want to offer friendship, support, and unconditional love. They will also want to encourage the individual to seek the services of one who can provide professional help as soon as possible. On campus, this may include the campus minister or student health services, both of whom will be aware of counseling services and community mental health agencies should they be needed.

11. Where can I get help with the development and continuation of our Covenant Discipleship group program?

The Covenant Discipleship group program is a part of the General Board of Discipleship of The United Methodist Church in Nashville, Tennessee. Printed resources are listed in Appendix I of this book. The Office of Covenant Discipleship in Nashville can also provide you with information about national and regional training events in the Covenant Discipleship Group program. Address your requests to the Covenant Discipleship Section, General Board of Discipleship of The United Methodist Church, P. O. Box 840, Nashville, TN 37202-0840.

Appendix I: Selected Resources

1. Resources for Covenant Discipleship Groups (available from Discipleship Resources, P. O. Box 189, Nashville, TN 37202; (615) 340-7284).

Covenant Discipleship: Christian Formation Through Mutual Accountability. This basic resource by David Lowes Watson provides the leader with essential historical and theological foundations of this early Methodist tradition, a step-by-step process by which to form Covenant Discipleship groups, and its implications for ministry today. (Order No. DR091B)

Branch Groups: Covenant Discipleship for Youth. This resource by Lisa Grant provides complete information about how to start Covenant Discipleship groups with youth in the local church. (Order No. DR067B)

Discípulos Responsables: Desarrolar Grupos de Discipulado Cristiano en la Iglesia Local. En este libro, el autor presenta una excelente base para la formación, desarrollo y acción de grupos de discípulos responsables en nuestra Iglesia. Por David Lowes Watson. Presentado por Mortimer Arias. (Numero F023B)

The Early Methodist Class Meeting: Its Origins and Significance. Written by David Lowes Watson, this basic resource introduces the modern reader to the early Methodist class meeting. Guidelines for using the class meeting in local congregations are also offered. (Order No. DR017B)

Covenant Discipleship Brochure. Explains the purpose and function of Covenant Discipleship groups. Available in sets of 100 only. Use as bulletin inserts and as "calling cards" for starting groups in your ministry. (Order No. M299L)

Covenant Discipleship Quarterly. A periodical containing articles about Covenant Discipleship groups throughout the nation as well as historical information and notices of regional and national

Covenant Discipleship meetings. (Order from Covenant Discipleship Section at the above address.)

2. Selected resources for devotional literature and faith development. These resources are available from Cokesbury, 201 Eighth
Avenue, South, Nashville, TN 37202. Telephone is toll-free to
order: 1-(800) 672-1789.

The Book of Discipline of The United Methodist Church. Parts I, II,
and III of *The Book of Discipline* include information on doctrinal
standards, the theological task, and the social principles of the
church.

Celebration of Discipline: The Path to Spiritual Growth. This book
by Richard J. Foster outlines the history and potential of a life of
discipline.

*Christian Spirituality: The Essential Guide to the Most Influential
Spiritual Writings of the Christian Tradition.* This excellent resource, edited by Frank N. Magill and Ian P. McGreal, presents a
collective vision of humanity's need for God's guidance.

The Upper Room Disciplines. This annual volume of devotions
includes a scripture reading, a brief commentary on the meaning
and application of the scripture, and a prayer or suggestion for
meditation for each day of the year. Its reasonable cost makes it a
good resource for every member of a college Covenant Discipleship
group. (Publisher: Upper Room Books)

A Guide to Prayer. Reuben P. Job and Norman Shawchuck wrote
this volume with includes devotions for throughout the church
year in weekly themes, with daily Bible readings from the lection-
ary. It also includes a superb collection of quotes from devotional
literature for each week's theme and orders for personal and group
retreats. (Publisher: Upper Room Books)

Journaling: A Spiritual Journey. Journaling as a method of spiritual discipline, written by Anne Broyles. (Publisher: Upper Room
Books)

The Practice of the Presence of God. Striving continuously to live and work in the presence of God, Brother Lawrence found the way to happiness in all circumstances and conditions. College students find this to be a fascinating and challenging approach to spirituality. (Various publishers)

Endnotes

1. David Lowes Watson, *Covenant Discipleship: Christian Formation Through Mutual Accountability* (Nashville: Discipleship Resources, 1991).
2. Edward Farley, *The Fragility of Knowledge: Theological Education in the Church and the University* (Philadelphia: Fortress Press, 1988), p. 60. Reprinted by permission of Augsburg Fortress.
3. Lisa Grant, *Branch Groups: Covenant Discipleship for Youth* (Nashville: Discipleship Resources, 1988), p. 1.
4. Watson, *Covenant Discipleship*.
5. The earliest New Testament writing is thought by scholars to be 1 Thessalonians, written in the early A.D. 50s. The first of the synoptic Gospels to be written was Mark, probably A.D. 65-70, more than thirty years after the death of Jesus.
6. Luke 5:16.
7. Mark 1:35.
8. Matthew 14:23.
9. John Dominic Crossan, *In Parables: The Challenge of the Historical Jesus* (New York: Harper and Row, 1973), p. 2.
10. Norman Perrin, *Rediscovering the Teaching of Jesus* (New York: Harper and Row, 1976).
11. Robin Maas, *Crucified Love: The Practice of Christian Perfection* (Nashville: Abingdon Press, 1989), p. 92. For a simple, elegant treatment of this metaphor in Christian perfection, see Chapter 5, "The Love of God and the Crucifixion of Self."
12. Notable was the little community of Herrnhut, where a remnant of the *Unitas Fratrum* flourished under the hospitality and protection of Count Nikolas Ludwig von Zinzendorf. Eventually the Moravian emphasis on personal spirituality came to view even good works as a potential obstacle to God. At this point the socially conscientious John Wesley and the Moravians parted company.
13. *The Rules of the United Societies* (1743) state: "There is one only Condition previously required, in those who desire Admission into these Societies, *a Desire to flee from the wrath to come, to be saved from their sins* (original emphasis): But wherever this is really fix'd in the Soul it will be shewn by its Fruits. It is therefore expected of all who continue therein, that they should continue to evidence their Desire of Salvation. . . ."
14. David Lowes Watson, *The Early Methodist Class Meeting* (Nashville: Discipleship Resources, 1985), p. 84. Despite the prescribed structure of the class meetings, in practice they seem to have been rather relaxed and supportive. According to one class member: "Problems were submitted and often solved, spiritual experiences were shared, and the members rejoiced in the conscious assurance of the presence of God. The meetings began and ended with a hymn and prayer, and there was simplicity and intimacy about the act of worship which any formalities would have destroyed." [Thomas Jackson, ed., *The Works of John Wesley* (Grand Rapids: Baker Book House, 1979), 5:357].
15. Watson, Ibid., p. 84.

16. Steve Harper, *Devotional Life in the Wesleyan Tradition* (Nashville: The Upper Room, 1983), p. 54.
17. Susanne Johnson, *Christian Spiritual Formation in the Church and Classroom* (Nashville: Abingdon Press, 1989), pp. 126-27. Used by permission.
18. See Watson, *Class Meeting*, pp. 137-38, 143 on the Halevy thesis; also see Clyde E. Fant, Jr. and William M. Pinson, Jr., eds., *Twenty Centuries of Great Preaching* (Waco, Texas: Word Books, 1971), 3:8: "Largely due to the influence of Wesley, between 1744 and 1784 the consumption of alcohol (in Britain) decreased remarkably."
19. "On Worldly Folly," 1790. Excerpted in Paul Wesley Chilcote, *Wesley Speaks on Christian Vocation* (Nashville: Discipleship Resources, 1986), p. 56.
20. Charles Wesley, "An Act of Devotion." Reprinted in *Covenant Discipleship Quarterly*, July, 1986, 1:1.
21. Watson, *Covenant Discipleship*.
22. Brother Lawrence, *The Practice of the Presence of God* (Nashville: Abingdon Press, 1975).
23. John 10:10.
24. Watson, *Class Meeting*, pp. 63-64.
25. Watson, *Covenant Discipleship*.
26. Perrin, *Rediscovering the Teaching of Jesus*.
27. Watson, *Class Meeting*, p. 120.
28. Ibid., p. 101.
29. Ibid., p. 142.
30. Watson, *Covenant Discipleship*.
31. I define "student ministry" as *ministry undertaken by a local church with students who attend that local church or are being recruited to participate in the programs of that particular local church*. Always a significant ministry to students, with the growth of the community colleges in our country, this becomes an *essential* ministry of the local church. Equally valid and essential to the church is "campus ministry," which is carried out by a clergy or layperson who is specially called to serve in ministry to the campus to students, faculty, administration, and support staff. Many campus ministry programs, therefore, take place on campus or in cooperation with Interreligious Councils in ecumenical and interfaith centers on campus, attempting to bring the concerns of the Christian faith to that setting. In this sense, campus ministry is the church's mission to the university. It is also evangelism as the Christian message is brought to the campus. The arguments that attempt to portray either local church student ministry or campus ministry as superior seem to be odd; both are needed. The eighteen- to thirty-year age group represents the largest percentage of dropouts among the entire church population. It would be unwise to think that any form of ministry with that age group is unnecessary.
32. Watson, *Covenant Discipleship*.
33. Other resources that can be used to begin Covenant Discipleship groups include the following guidebooks: David Lowes Watson, *Covenant Discipleship: Christian Formation Through Mutual Accountability* (Discipleship Resources: Nashville, TN, 1991), and Lisa Grant, *Branch Groups: Covenant Discipleship for Youth* (Discipleship Resources: Nashville, TN, 1988).

    Additional helpful information can be found in the following: David Lowes Watson, *The Early Methodist Class Meeting* (Discipleship Resources: Nashville, TN, 1985). This book includes sections on John Wesley's theology of discipleship and the significance of the class meeting for accountable discipleship in the early Methodist class meeting.

Covenant Discipleship Quarterly, a periodical published each quarter by the Covenant Discipleship section of the General Board of Discipleship in Nashville, TN. The quarterly includes articles about Covenant Discipleship group training events, the experiences of Covenant Discipleship groups around the country, and articles from a historical perspective.

34. Watson, *Class Meeting,* pp. 99, 101.
35. Ibid., p. 151.
36. Watson, *Covenant Discipleship.*
37. Ibid.
38. Ibid.
39. Ibid.
40. Ibid.
41. Ibid.